stage lighting
THE TECHNICIANS' GUIDE
2nd edition

an on-the-job reference tool
plus online video resources

SKIP MORT

Bloomsbury Methuen Drama

An imprint of Bloomsbury Publishing Plc

Imprint previously known as Methuen Drama

50 Bedford Square	1385 Broadway
London	New York
WC1B 3DP	NY 10018
UK	USA

www.bloomsbury.com

BLOOMSBURY, METHUEN DRAMA and the Diana logo are trademarks of Bloomsbury Publishing Plc

Second edition published 2015

British Library Cataloguing-in-Publication Data.
A catalogue record for this book is available from the British Library.

ISBN: PB: 978-1-4742-1270-0
ePDF: 978-1-4742-1272-4
epub: 978-1-4742-1271-7

Library of Congress Cataloging-in-Publication Data
A catalog record for this book is available from the Library of Congress

Typeset by Fakenham Prepress Solutions, Fakenham, Norfolk NR21 8NN
Printed and bound in India

stage lighting
THE TECHNICIANS' GUIDE
2nd edition

an on-the-job reference tool
plus online video resources

SKIP MORT

Bloomsbury Methuen Drama
An imprint of Bloomsbury Publishing Plc

B L O O M S B U R Y
LONDON • NEW DELHI • NEW YORK • SYDNEY

Stage Lighting – The Technicians' Guide
For Maurice and David

CONTENTS

Foreword for the first edition   vi
Foreword for the second edition   vii
Acknowledgements   viii
Introduction   x

PART ONE: ## Lighting Technician   1

Lanterns, Dimmers & Control – getting down
to basics   3

Colour, Gobos & Effects – some useful
additions   135

PART TWO: ## Lighting Designer   211

Lighting the Performance Space – getting
started   213

Lighting the Show – from page to stage   275

PART THREE: ## Lighting Resources   347

Online Video Resources   349

Technical info.   351

Websites   378

Key notes!   381

Credits   384

Bibliography   386

Index   389

The First Edition:

Stage Lighting – The Technicians' Guide is a very practical and useful book for beginners setting up a lighting system for a performance, and, for those already working in lighting, it is a very handy reference. The helpful layout allows you to quickly find the specific information you need, and then provides the necessary background knowledge along with suggestions for further reading. It always relates method to results, and not only explains the 'how', but also gives insight into the 'why'. It also contains useful explanations of terminology (as well as international variants for specialist terms).

The job of the technician and lighting designer is to utilise the vast amount of technology, both new and old, to produce what can often be perceived as 'invisible' stage lighting (and, in some cases, it is deliberately very overt). *The Technicians' Guide* demonstrates how to successfully achieve this objective alongside a safe working practice. It also helps people with a technical background to create their first designs.

The Technicians' Guide points the reader to current websites updated by manufacturers and trade bodies, so they can be sure that they are able to access information about the latest equipment and practices.

Lighting is a delicate combination of technical craft and artistic skill. A lighting designer or technician needs to understand how different effects and moods are created by subtle differences in the way light relates to performers and stage environments and how this is perceived in the eyes and minds of the audience. *The Technicians' Guide* will certainly help those working in this wonderfully emotive medium to achieve skilful and artistic results.

Rick Fisher; Lighting Designer

The Second Edition:

The best teacher is a mix of education, experience, and re-training; education lays the foundation of understanding, experience builds on that foundation and re-training repairs the cracks in the foundation caused by advancing technology. Two of the keys to getting a great education are an insatiable thirst for knowledge and the right tools to dip deep into the well of information.

The more technology changes, the greater the need for updated information. The second edition of *Stage Lighting: The Technicians' Guide* reflects the latest changes in the field of stage lighting, most notably the rapid advancement of LED technology and its effects. In addition to describing different types of LED luminaires and how each of them work, Skip Mort describes some of the pros and cons of LED lighting, as well as how the increased use of non-generic luminaires has affected the more traditional practices related to power distribution, dimming and switching, distribution of data, on-board dimming and more. He also includes updates on the practice of programming using color palettes, color matching, and other aspects affected by today's LED and automated-lighting luminaires.

LEDs aren't the only technology that has been making great strides. Basically, anything with a computer chip in it is rapidly advancing. This edition features updated information about lighting desks, automated lights, digital projection, and media servers, as well as CAD programs and automated lighting rigs. There is also new material about one of the most relevant and important topics today – health and safety – as well as interesting titbits about stage lighting history, expanded Global Jargon sections, updated technical information on lanterns, dimmers, and control, and an updated lighting resources website directory.

I know how hard Skip Mort worked on this book because we exchanged several emails during the course of the revision. But you don't have to be on the inside to feel his passion for the book, the subject material, and the industry. Whether you're a teacher looking for a text to use, a student looking for the answers to your many questions, or a professional seeking to advance your understanding and your career, you will enjoy the second edition of *Stage Lighting: The Technicians' Guide*.

Richard Cadena; Lighting Designer

Author, and founder of the Academy of Production Technology USA, Technical editor PLASA Media – Lighting & Sound America, Lighting & Sound International.

2 Dimmers

Generic lanterns[1] are controlled by a dimmer unit. These are electronic devices that control the level or intensity of light produced by the lantern. The individual dimmer units are mounted in modular racks or portable packs.

Beta Pack – Zero88

3 Control

The dimmer units are controlled by miniature sliding faders on the lighting control desk. The desk may be positioned away from the dimmers as a remote control so that the operator can see clearly the action of the drama. Memory desks can be programmed to control DMX fixtures moving lights and LED fixtures.

Smartfade lighting desk – ETC

> **Online video link – 1.1: Understanding the lighting system**
> https://vimeo.com/123717415

Two types of dimmer systems

Dimmer racks

➤ **Hardwired systems use dimmer racks**

On permanent hardwired installations, the electrical wiring from the circuit outlet sockets is contained in metal trunking or conduit and connected direct to the dimmer units. The sockets are distributed throughout the stage and auditorium.

- **Studio or small stage installations** – the circuits are usually terminated in sockets on or above fixed lighting bars or terminated at stage/floor level for side lighting
- **Internally Wired Bars (IWBs)** are used on installations in the UK. The circuit outlet sockets are mounted directly on the bar with the cables running internally
- **Circuit outlet sockets** may be paired together and wired direct to the same dimmer control channel
- **Larger stages and installations** the dimmer circuits may be terminated in outlet patch panels mounted

Chilli Dimmer Rack – Zero88

[1] See Lanterns-performance luminaires

A quick start

1 FROM LANTERN TO CONTROL

adjacent to the lighting bars that are suspended from the flying grid. The outlet sockets on the bars are connected by a multicore cable ending with a 'spider'[2] of flexible cables terminated in plug tops which are hard patched into the dimmer outlet patch panel

■ **Fixed wired outlet sockets** on lighting bars or dimmer outlet patch panels are usually numbered by the dimmer circuit/channel fader number that is controlling them

➤ **Using a hardwired system**

A lantern connected to circuit outlet socket No.1 on the bar or dimmer outlet patch panel will be controlled by dimmer No.1 and channel fader No.1 on the lighting desk programmed with a 1:1 soft patch (see 'Lighting jargon – Lighting control desks').

Dimmer packs

➤ **Hard patch systems use dimmer packs**

Dimmer packs consist of six dimmer units mounted in a portable rack. Each dimmer unit has a single or pair of outlet sockets mounted either on the front or back providing the flexibility to hard patch any lantern to any dimmer. They are used for small stages and studio installations and for temporary rigs in the UK, Europe and the Southern Hemisphere.

Dimmer pack & cable patch – GMSL

■ The circuit outlet sockets on the bars are hardwired back to a cable patch being terminated in flexible cables with numbered plug tops

■ The cable patch is mounted below the dimmer packs allowing the individual circuit outlet sockets on the bars to be hard patched to any of the dimmer units

■ Hard patching makes it possible to have a larger number of circuit outlet sockets than the number of dimmer units so that they can be widely distributed over the lighting bars and at floor level. This provides a greater flexibility to position the lanterns anywhere in the rig without the need for additional cabling

■ Lanterns can be paired together but care must be taken to prevent overloading the individual dimmer units

■ Hard patching is used on temporary lighting rigs for shows where flexible cables are used to connect the lanterns to the dimmer units. In North America, this is called 'hooking up'

[2] See 'Lighting jargon – Lanterns performance luminaires' page 129

➤ **Using a hard patching system**

A lantern hanging on a lighting bar is plugged into a circuit outlet socket No.12 which is terminated with a matching numbered plug top at the cable patch. If plug top No.12 is connected or patched to dimmer unit No.1, the lantern will then be controlled by channel fader No.1 on the lighting control desk.[3] The lantern and the area of lighting will now be called by the same channel fader number, No.1.

Did you know that –

■ Lantern or 'Lanthorn' is an early English name for a source of light enclosed in a housing as used by William Shakespeare in his plays[4]

■ 'Magic lantern' was the term used for the early glass slide projectors as used in Victorian and Edwardian times in the UK

■ Bunches of cables taped together from a lighting bar are traditionally called 'tripe' in the UK and the 'Snake' in North America as they describe what they look like

■ 'Socapex' and 'Lectriflex' are names frequently used for multicores named after the make and type of the multipin plugs or sockets used to terminate the multicore

■ 'Soco' is a term used in North America for a multicore cable

GLOBAL JARGON

■ **Lanterns** (United Kingdom/UK) – **Fixtures**, **Instruments**, **Units**, (North America/NA)

■ **Fittings & Fixtures** – also used in UK, Fixtures relating to moving lights

■ **Luminaires** (Northern Europe/NE) – International term, also used in North America(NA) & Southern Hemisphere (NZ & Aus)

■ **Spotlights** (NE) – Fresnels and PCs

■ **Patching** (UK) – **Hooking up** (NA)

■ **Lamps** – Light source not a stage light or lantern

---

[3] That is, providing the lighting control desk is on a 1:1 default patch. See soft patching, Chapter 5 'Lighting control – Extras!' page 90

[4] *The Art of Stage Lighting*, Frederick Bentham

QUICK TIPS

■ The lanterns are always called by the channel fader number that they are controlled by

■ When planning the areas of lighting, it is easier to remember and recall them if they are in a logical sequence

■ Number the areas as viewed from the front from 'House Left to Right' (Stage Right to Left), e.g. 1–3 across stage and 4–6 behind

■ When using a hard patching system, patch the lanterns lighting an area to the same numbered channel fader but check that the total load doesn't exceed the capacity of the dimmer unit

■ Record the channel fader number that is controlling the lantern in front of the symbol on the lighting plan

■ Record the circuit outlet socket number that is connecting the lantern to the dimmer unit on a hard patch plan so that you can easily identify faults

Points for action

Quickies!

■ Try your lighting system out – flash through[5] the lanterns that are hanging and see if you can relate the control channel fader to the lanterns and the areas that they are lighting

Takes longer

■ Make a simple sketch plan of the areas that the existing lanterns are lighting and number them according to the channel fader numbers

A proper job!

■ Make a lighting plan of the position of the lighting bars, outlet sockets and their numbers

■ Mark the position of the lanterns on the plan use the CIE symbols, see Chapter 2 'Lanterns – performance luminaires'

■ Flash through the lanterns and record the channel fader number in the lantern symbol on the plan

[5] See 'Lighting jargon – Lighting control desks'

2 Lanterns – performance luminaires

A quick start – Identifying lanterns

Looking at the five types of generic lanterns: Floods, Parcans, Fresnels, PCs/Prism/Pebble & Plano-convex, Profiles, the characteristics of the beams, where to use them, makes of lanterns and models

More info – Adjusting lanterns

Angling and focusing the lanterns, adjusting and shaping beams, lantern accessories and adding colour

Extras! – How do they work?

Looking at the optical system of the five types of generic lanterns

A quick start – Identifying lanterns

There are three groups of lighting units or fixtures: generic lanterns, automated or moving lights and LED fixtures. Generic lantern is a term given to a fixed luminaire, which is a lantern that is manually positioned and focused. There are five different types of generic lanterns and they each have a distinct quality of beam of light that are used for different purposes.

Five types of tungsten source generic lanterns:
Floods – Parcans – Fresnels – PC Prism Convex – Profiles

The lanterns can be divided into two main groups:

- **Fixed beam lanterns** – having a lamp and reflector
- **Focus lanterns** – having a lens system to adjust the focus and or the size of the beam

> **❯** **Online video link – 2.1: Five types of lanterns**
> https://vimeo.com/123717416

9

Five types of lanterns – five different beams of light

Lanterns can be identified by the:

- Shape of the body housing
- Type of lens system or reflector
- Quality of the beam of light produced

➤ Fixed beam lanterns – tungsten

90° Flood – symmetric

Hui Flood – Philips Selecon

Symmetrical Reflector

- **Soft edged wash** – fixed beam providing an even intense flood of light with minimal spill
- **Use** – overhead washes, traditionally used for lighting door and window backings
- **Position** – on-stage: overhead and on lighting stands

Cyc Flood – asymmetric

Hui Cyc – Philips Selecon

Asymmetrical Reflector

- **Soft edged wash** – fixed beam size, soft evenly distributed wash on to a vertical surface
- **Use** – lighting cycloramas or skycloths with coloured light, can be either single or joined together in banks of 3 or 4 units to provide colour mixing. Also used for lighting back cloths, scenery and curtains
- **Position** – on-stage: rear overhead & floor cyc positions or front stage as footlights

◖ Parcans

PAR lamp – GMSL

Parcan – Thomas Eng

- **Sealed beam PAR lamp** – a lamp containing a filament with a **P**arabolic **A**luminium **R**eflector and lens in a sealed unit
- **Parallel beam of light** – intense near parallel oval beam of light that can be rotated
- **Use** – narrow or wide shafts of light, downlighting, side and back lighting. Good for use with strong, saturated colours. Light in weight, easy to angle, no focusing required, originally designed for pop concerts
- **Position** – on-stage: overhead, side and rear stage, floor & special effects

➤ Focus lanterns – tungsten

▯ Fresnel

Fresnel lens – GMSL

Acclaim Fresnel – Philips Selecon

- **Fresnel lens** – concentric stepped lens, each step having a flat and convex surface
- **Soft edged beam** – evenly distributed, diffused beam having a soft shadow edge producing scatter/spill light
- **Use** – large areas from a short throw distance, used for area, side and back lighting. Soft scatter light helps blend overlapping beams to create smooth washes
- **Position** – on-stage: overhead, side and rear stage
- **Lantern body** – Selecon Acclaim same as PC but shorter

PC – Prism Convex

Prism-convex lens – GMSL

Acclaim PC – Philips Selecon

Plano-convex lens – GMSL

Arena PC 2000/2500W – Philips Selecon

- **Prism/Pebble-convex lens** – Plano-convex lens cast with a prism/stippled on the flat surface softening the edge of the beam
- **Semi-hard/semi-soft edged beam** – a 'crisp' intense beam with smaller amount of spill light than the Fresnel, soft edged beam is good for blending areas of light
- **Use** – small or large areas of light, long or short throws of light, used for specials, acting areas or washes and side lighting
- **Position** – on-stage: overhead, side stage
- **Lantern body** – Selecon Acclaim same as the Fresnel but longer

- **Plano-convex lens** having a highly polished flat surface available in 1K, 2K & 2.5K lanterns
- **Sharp edged beam** – zoom beam with no spill light, shaping limited to barndoors
- **Use** – controlled beam of light suitable for projecting over longer throws an alternative to using Profile spots – quick to focus
- **Position** – FOH lighting (mainly used in Europe), on-stage: overhead, side stage

A quick start

2 LANTERNS – PERFORMANCE LUMINAIRES

⊖ Profile spot

Plano-convex lens – GMSL

SPX Ellipsoidal – Philips Selecon

Pacfic base-down Ellipsoidal – Philips Selecon

Source Four CE – ETC

- **Plano-convex lens** having one curved and one flat surface
- **Hard edge/soft focused, precise beam** – an optical spotlight having a beam that can be accurately shaped or 'profiled' with very little spill light
- **Use** – controlled beam of light suitable for projecting over longer throws and lighting precise areas, images and patterns can be projected with the use of gobos
- **Position** – Front of House 'FOH', on-stage: overhead, side stage

3.5Q Ellipsoidal – Altman Lighting

Generic lantern symbol stencil – White Light

2 LANTERNS – PERFORMANCE LUMINAIRES **A quick start**

Basic lantern symbols

Basic lantern symbols – GMSL

The CIE basic lantern symbols provide a simple and easy way of recording the type and positions of lanterns on lighting layout plans. The symbols are based on simplified images of the five generic types of lanterns and are easy to use as they can be drawn by hand or reproduced on basic computer drawing programs.

For generic lantern stencils, see 'Quick resources'.

Did you know that –

■ Focus Lamps or Lanterns were the first theatre spotlights to be developed in the 1890s by adapting the basic optical system used for 'Limelights' and adding an incandescent lamp. They worked in a similar way to the Fresnel/PC, having a movable light source with a reflector and a Plano-convex lens that gave an uneven distribution of light across the beam creating a rainbow effect on the edge

■ The Strand Patt 43A 1000W Batten spot, Patt 44 500W Baby spot and Patt 45 250W Miniature spot were developed in the 1930s, having a Plano-convex lens and spherical reflector that tended to project the pattern of the lamp's filament

■ The Fresnel lens was first developed by Augustine Fresnel (1788–1827) for use in lighthouses and it is named after its designer and pronounced with a silent s, 'Frenel'

■ The Fresnel focus spot was developed from the focus lantern by changing the lens, adding a reflector to increase the output and the quality of the beam of light

■ In 1981, the PC/Prism-convex lantern was introduced to the new Strand Prelude range of lanterns replacing the Plano-convex lens of the focus lantern with the newly developed Prism-convex lens

■ In North America, PCs are not commonly used or sold by theatre lighting companies

■ PCs with Plano-convex lenses are used in Europe for FOH lighting as an alternative to Profile spots

■ The CIE symbol used for the Profile spot is based on the shape of the original Strand Patt. 23 lantern but that's a bit of history!

■ 'In the film business, PAR lamps are known as "bird's eyes" after the alleged inventor Clarence Birdseye'[6]

[6] A Glossary of Technical Theatre Terms – www.theatrecraft.com

Different makes & models of lanterns

Lanterns are a bit like cars in that each manufacturer produces their own distinctive design model and name for their range of each of the five types of generic lanterns.

➤ **Makes of lanterns**

Some lanterns tend to be mainly used in the country where they are manufactured, while others are used worldwide:

Country of manufacture	Makes of lanterns
United Kingdom	**Philips Selecon** (distributed by **Philips Strand** in the UK) – **Thomas** – **CCT** (used in the education market) **Strand** (no longer manufactured but still in use)
Europe	**ADB** (Belgium) – **Robert Juliat** (France) – **Spotlight, Coemar** – **Teatro Teclum** (Italy)
North America	**Altman** – **ETC** (used in UK & Europe) – **James Thomas** – **Strand Century** (no longer manufactured but still in use)
Southern Hemisphere	**Philips Selecon** (New Zealand, widely used in UK and Europe)

Lanterns wattage & models

➤ **Power/wattage of lanterns**

The models can also be grouped together by their power/wattage of the lamp used in the lantern which affects the light output, throw and use. Watts are a measurement of electrical energy or power used by the lamp and they indicate the quantity of light produced by the lantern.[7]

- Lantern wattages range from:
  500/650W – 575/600W – 750W – 800W – 1000/1.200W (1/1.2kW) – 2.000/2.500W (2/2.5kW)

➤ **Models of lanterns**

Manufacturers identify their generic lanterns in a number of ways, e.g.:

- Some use the wattage and the generic name – **650W Fresnel**
- Others link the name of the model to the wattage – **Acclaim Fresnel, PC** (650W range)
- Profiles are often identified by their beam angle – **Acclaim Axial 18-34** (8°–34°)
- Some are identified by the diameter of the lens – **Alt. 6" Profile**

---

[7] See Chapter 4 'Dimmers'

Wattage	Model name	Throw	Use
500/650 watts	Acclaim, Alt. 6" Fresnel, Coda, Combi, Minuette, Prelude, Quartet	Short	Small stages & drama studios
575/600 watts	*Axial Profiles:* Acclaim, Alt. 6" Ellipsoidal, Pacific, SL, Source Four, Shakespeare, Warp *NB The advanced optical system & lamp source produces a powerful beam of light*	Medium	Medium auditoriums & larger stages
750 watts	*Axial Profiles:* Ellipsoidal, Pacific, Source Four *Equivalent output to former 2000/2500W Profiles*	Long	Larger auditoriums & stages
800 watts	*Axial Profile:* Pacific, Warp	Long	Larger auditoriums & stages
1000 watts	*Axial Profile:* Leko, Pacific, Silhouette *Fresnel –* Alt. 8", Lutin, Rama	Long	Larger auditoriums Medium to large stages
1000/1200 watts 1Kw/1.2kW	Cantata, Combi, Compact, Europe, Harmony, Rama, R&J 600 R&J SX, Sintesi, Starlette	Medium	Medium to large stages Medium auditoriums
2000/2500 watts 2kW/2.5kW	Alto, Arena, Europe, Evolution, R&J 700SX2, Sintesi, Evolution, Starlette	Long	Large theatres

- Some of the above models of lanterns are no longer being made but you may still find them in current use for hire or in educational establishments
- **R&J –** Robert Juliat, **Alt.** – Altman Lighting

Makes & models of lanterns – a quick guide

See part 3 Lighting Resources – Technical Info page 351

Did you know that –

- Older lanterns were originally designed to take 500W and 1000 watt lamps; equivalent modern lanterns now use 650W and 1200 watt lamps
- Strand Electric lanterns originally called their lanterns by their Patent or Pattern numbers
- In 1953, the Patt 23 was the first die cast 500 watt 'baby Profile' spotlight in the world to be mass produced by Strand Electric, closely followed by the Patt 123 Fresnel
- They were produced in batches of 5000s for a market in which a gross (144) was considered to be an outsized batch[8]
- 500,000 Patt 23s were produced by 1983 and they can still be found in use worldwide
- Strand first introduced zoom lenses in 1981 to the 1000w Harmony and then in 1983 to the 500w Prelude Profile spot
- Strand Electric was founded in 1914 and it is the oldest UK stage lighting company. It was originally formed to service the London West End theatres, having its offices at 29 King Street, Covent Garden
- Strand Lighting was formed in 1968 with the purchase of the company by the Rank Organisation, also taking over Century Lighting in New York, acquiring Vari-Lite and the Italian Quartzcolour
- Strand Lighting was bought in the late 1990s by venture capitalists and then in 2006 it was acquired by the Genlyte Group who were purchased in 2008, becoming part of the Royal Philips Lighting group along with Selecon Performance Lighting in 2009
- Philips Strand Lighting now produce dimmers and controls and Philips Selecon produce lanterns

QUICK TIPS

- A safety bond must be used when hanging a lantern to provide a secondary suspension
- Safety bonds have now replaced the use of safety chains in the UK as they are required to be load tested
- Parcans – to adjust the position of the oval beam, rotate the lamp housing knob on the end of the lantern
- Parcans are called after the name of the Parabolic Aluminium Reflector (PAR) lamp which is used in the lantern
- Theatre lamps have a short life and are expensive to replace; don't use them as working lights

---

[8] 'Phillips Strand Lighting' Lighting and Sound International

Profile spots – shaping & adjusting the beam

The beam of light on a Profile spot can be accurately shaped or Profiled at the 'Gate' of the lantern which is at the central point of focus between the reflector & lamp tray and the lens system.

➤ **Four rotating shutters** or 'Cuts' can be used to produce an accurate angular, rectangular or diamond shape. As you slide the shutters in, they produce a straight edge on the opposite side of the projected circular beam of light. They can be rotated to line up with any obstruction to remove or 'cut' unwanted parts of the circular beam of light overshooting the edge of the stage, the proscenium arch, the edge of a piece of scenery or the masking.

Profile shutters – GMSL

➤ **Gobos** are thin stainless steel discs with a pattern etched through the surface. It is mounted in a gobo holder that is inserted into the gate, a slot in the centre of the body of a Profile spot. Gobos are used to project an image on to the stage floor, backcloth or scenery.
NB The gobo image is mounted upside down as the optical system reverses the projected image.

Inserting a Gobo holder – GMSL

➤ **Irises** are used on fixed lens Profile spots to change the size of the beam of light as the beam size cannot be adjusted optically as on a zoom spot. They are also used in follow spots where the size of the beam needs to be manually controlled by the operator.

Inserting an Iris – GMSL

➤ **Flat/Peak field of light adjustment***
The characteristics of the beam of light can be altered from 'peak' to 'flat' beam by finely adjusting the position of the lamp filament relative to the reflector.

■ **Peak beam** gives a central hot spot falling off evenly to the edges of the beam. This setting provides an even cover on the overlap between the areas on a wash of light on-stage

* Beam adjustment see pages 27, 28, 29

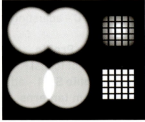

Peak/Flat beam distribution – Philips Selecon

(side margin) **2 LANTERNS – PERFORMANCE LUMINAIRES   More info**

■ **Flat beam** setting provides an evenly spread beam of light suitable for projecting gobos

➤ **Donuts** are metal masking plates with a circular cut-out that are inserted into the gate of Ellipsoidal spotlights to increase the clarity of projected gobo patterns by reducing halation and sharpening the image.

Donuts – Apollo Design Technology Inc.

➤ **Snoots or top hats** are "devices used in theatrical lighting to shield the audience's eyes from the direct source of the light. It is shaped like a top hat with a hole in the top and the brim being inserted into the colour frame guides on the front of a Profile, Axial or Parcan lanterns. The light passes through the cylinder removing any reflected light from the lantern and reduces any flare or spill lighting from the immediate auditorium architecture.

'This is very useful when lanterns are hung near the proscenium arch or other objects that the designer doesn't want to light.'[9]

Tophat – Apollo Design Technology, Inc.

Did you know that –

■ The shutters on the original profiles Strand Patt 23s, 263 and 16–30s only rotated through 90° unlike the almost 360° on modern lanterns. The Patt 264 and 774 had two sets of hard and soft shutters

PCs & Fresnels – Shaping the beam

➤ **Barndoors** are used to shape the beam of light on a PC or Fresnel. They are inserted into the first set of colour runners on the front of the lantern and held in place by a spring clip or by the lift-up top on the colour runner box. They have hinged metal doors that can be rotated and angled in order to shape the beam, reduce the scatter/spill light or mask the overshoot on to scenery or masking.

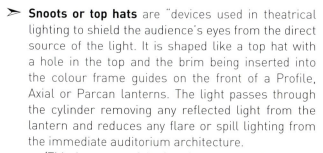

Barndoors – Philips Selecon

[9] Wikipedia, the free encyclopedia

Lanterns makes & models – see Part 3: 'Lighting Resources – Technical info.'

Lantern design

The development of the optical systems for lanterns has always been dependent on the production of the appropriate lamp sources. Traditionally in the UK, lamps were designed to be used 'base down' at 90 degrees to the central axis of the lantern.

➤ **1930s** – Elliposidal reflector spotlights were developed using 110 volt 'base-up' lamp. They were widely used in North America but the low-voltage lamps greatly restricted their use in countries where 240 volt power supplies were in use in the UK, Europe and the Southern Hemisphere.

➤ **1953** – Strand Electric Patt 23 Profile & Patt 123 Fresnel first die-cast lantern using a 250/500W T1 lamp. Patt 23 was produced with interchangeable lens, Fresnel, Wide and a Narrow lens tube. Also a 23S with four shutters having 90 degree rotation with a square rather than circular gate.

Patt 23 – Strand Electric

➤ **1960s** – Strand Lighting developed an Ellipsoidal Profile using a 240 volt, T4 1000 watt 'base-up' lamp. The Patt 264 bifocal spotlight had hard and soft edged shutters with a throw of 10m and was widely used in the UK.

➤ **1970s** – Altman Lighting introduced the 360Q Axial Ellipsoidal Reflector Spotlight the first Axial lantern having the lamp filament positioned along the optical axis of the lantern.

➤ **1990s** – Further developments in the development of Axial lanterns with the availability of the compact tungsten filament allowing the lamp to be mounted along the central axis of an elliptical reflector and the optical system.

Patt 264 – Strand Electric

■ The development of the 570/600 Watt HPL lamp with a 'Compact' filament created a more efficient optical system. This produced a powerful 'Whiter' light equivalent to 1000 Watt conventional lamps giving a 40% energy saving. See 'Comparing current requirements' page 70 'Dimmers Extras!'.

■ The concept of 'Cool' lanterns was created by the development of the dichroic-coated glass 'hot' mirror that reflects 90% of the infrared radiation wave lengths of light to the heat management system at the back of the lantern.

Source Four – ETC

Did you know that –

- In 1933, the first Ellipsoidal spotlight was developed by Century Lighting in North America and was called 'Leko' or 'Lekolite' after the first half of the surnames of its inventors Joseph Levy and Edward Kook
- In the 1970s, Zoom spots or 'Zoomers' having an adjustable beam size were developed and used in North America
- The Strand Patt 23 profile was a forerunner having an interchangeable 11° long focus lens for the standard 22°
- In 1992, David Cunningham designs the ETC Source Four applying the advances in compact filament lamps and reflector technology to increase light output with reduced wattage.
- It was designed to use a wide range of interchangeable lens tubes, allowing a single body to use a multiple of beam field angles ranging from 5° to 90°. Source Four is a popular lantern with international lighting designers
- Zoom Axial Profiles are now more widely used in Europe and the UK, especially in drama studios and medium-sized theatres where flexibility is an important requirement
- Lighting designers ETC Source Four was designed around the High Performance HPL lamp having a compact four stranded filament hence the name *'Source Four'* having zoom lenses/Zoomers
- The lamp on a Source Four Fresnel is mounted axially and not like other Fresnels at 90° to the central axis

EXTRA TIPS

- Flat & peak field adjustment – angle the lantern at a white wall 4–8 metres away, focus light to a narrow sharp focused beam, carefully adjust the position of the lamp tray/housing to move the filament. NB the filament will be burning at white heat and it can be easily damaged
- 90 degree Ellipsoidal lanterns can be used for back lighting instead of Fresnels. They have a similar light output with the beam control of a Profile and the option to use gobo break-ups
- ETC Source Four & Selecon Pacific lanterns have a range of 11 interchangeable lens tubes which can be fitted with beam angles ranging from 5 to 90 degrees. The barrel/lens tubes can be rotated for the accurate alignment of projected gobos

More resources – go to
www.altmanltg.com – Altman Stage Lighting: NA
www.adblighting.com – ADB Lighting Technologies: Belgium
www.cctlighting.com – CCT Lighting: UK
www.etcconnect.com – ETC: NA
www.seleconlight.com – Philips Selecon: New Zealand
www.robertjuliat.fr – Robert Juliat: France
www.spotlight.it – Spotlight Italy
www.strandarchive.co.uk – Strand Lighting archive
www.jthomaseng.com – James Thomas Engineering: UK
www.teclumen.it – Teatro Teclumen: Italy

Extras!

2 LANTERNS – PERFORMANCE LUMINAIRES

3 Working with lanterns

A quick start – Rigging lanterns

Good working practice, hanging, angling & focusing, striking lanterns and accessories

More info – Lantern maintenance

Maintaining lanterns, troubleshooting and replacing lamps

Extras! – Electrical safety

Introduction to the requirements of electrical testing, user checks, what to do if you find a fault

A quick start – Rigging lanterns

Good working practices help to create a safe working environment and can save a lot of time when working on-stage so it is worth finding out the right way to do things.

Good working practice

Hanging lanterns

Lanterns are hung from lighting bars on hanging clamps by a suspension bolt that is attached to the lantern stirrup/hanging bracket. The lantern should have a safety bond/wire attaching it to the bar for safety in case the primary suspension fails, e.g. suspension bolt or hook clamp.

Lantern suspension – GMSL

➤ **Preparing the equipment – checklist**
Before you start to rig the lanterns, check the following points:

☑ **The hanging clamp is correctly fitted** above the hanging stirrup so as not to restrict the movement of the lantern

☑ **The suspension bolt is tight** in the stirrup to prevent any addition movement once the lantern has been set in position

A quick start

3 WORKING WITH LANTERNS

✓ **The safety bond/wire** is permanently attached to the anchor point on the lantern; see 'More info'

➤ ## Checking the electrical safety of the equipment
A visual check should be made by the user every time a lantern or extension cable is used. This is an important safety precaution as many faults can be identified providing you know what to look for.

PAT sticker – GMSL

Cable socket – GMSL

Check the equipment to ensure that:

✓ **The lantern has been PAT tested** in the last 12 months – check the date on the green test sticker on the lantern

✓ **The lantern cable** is securely held at the point of entry to the body of the lantern and to the cable plug

✓ **Flexible extension cables have been PAT tested**, the cable is free from damage and securely held at the point of entry to the cable plug, socket/connector. That the live and neutral connections on 15 amp flexible cable socket are protected by red sprung shutters

✓ **Do not use the equipment** if it hasn't been PAT tested or if there are any obvious visual electrical faults

Damaged cable – GMSL

Portable Appliance Testing, see Chapter 3 'Working with lanterns – Extras!'

Rigging

It is important to do the things in the right order to hang the lanterns correctly, also to check that the lighting plan is the right way round.

✓ **Hanging lanterns** – check the following points:

✓ **The lantern stirrup** is hanging in vertical position and not at an angle; see 'Quick tips'

✓ **The hanging clamp is tight** on the bar

✓ **The lantern is hanging the right way up** with the cable entry at the bottom

✓ **The safety bond is attached over the bar** allowing the lantern to fully rotate

✓ **The lantern cable is looped loosely over the bar** allowing the lantern to move freely

✓ **The lantern movement** is free to rotate from side to side and tilt up and down

The lantern has enough space – roughly angle it in the right direction to check that it will do what you want it to do and isn't restricted by other lanterns

✓ **Spot focus the lantern** in preparation for focusing

✓ **Colour frames & barndoors** are safely attached to prevent them falling out when the lantern is tilted

✓ **Open up barndoors and shutters on Profile spots** so that you can see that the lantern is working when it is 'flashed through'

✓ **The lantern cable is not fixed or taped to the bar** to allow easy removal if a fault occurs

✓ **Extension cables being used are the right length**; too long or too short can cause a safety hazard also that they will not be damaged by some mechanical movement, e.g. pinched under a door

Hanging a lantern –
Philips Selecon

> ❯ **Online video link – 3.1: Adjusting Lanterns**
> https://vimeo.com/123717417

Focusing lanterns – 'Hitting your spot!'

When you are focusing, position yourself directly behind the lantern.

➤ **Angling the lantern**
- **'Spot focus'** the beam adjustment
- **'Turn, Slacken, Slide & Tighten'** the adjustment knob to move the lens or lamp housing and to fix the setting
- **'Pan and Tilt'** the lantern so the middle of the beam hits between the neck and shoulders of the person standing in the centre of the area to be lit
- **'Lock off'** tightening the hanging bolt and pivoting wing bolts to prevent any further movement

➤ **Focusing the lantern**
PCs & Fresnels
- **Open up the beam** of light slowly to the required size to light the area
- **Shape the beam** of light, adjusting the barndoors to remove any unwanted scatter or spill light from the set or masking

➤ **Profile spots**
- **Zoom Profiles adjust size** – by moving the front lens adjustment knob
- **Hard or soft focus** the edge of the beam as required using the rear lens adjustment on zoom Profiles (on some lanterns it can be easier to adjust both lenses together)
- **Shape the beam** of light using the four rotating shutters or 'cuts' to remove or cut the unwanted light from proscenium arch, front of stage or off parts of the set

3 WORKING WITH LANTERNS

A quick start

➤ **Saving your lamps**

Take care when angling and focusing lanterns. The lamps are expensive to replace, they only have a relatively short life and the tungsten filament is very fragile.

- **Set the dimmer level at 90%** or point 9 when focusing to reduce the possibility of the filament breaking
- **Handle lantern carefully** when you are adjusting it as the tungsten filament in the lamp burns at white heat and it can be easily broken
- **'Save your lamps!'** – fade out each lantern when you have finished focusing it to remove unwanted light and to prevent it becoming too hot too handle

De-rigging lanterns

Strike the lanterns in the following order to prevent damage and ending up in a mess.

➤ **Lanterns checklist:**

Step 1
- ✓ **Switch off the lantern**
- ✓ **Unplug the lantern and coil the cable**

Step 2
- ✓ **Profile spots** – close the shutters to prevent them being bent
- ✓ **PCs & Fresnels** – close the barndoors
- ✓ **Swing the lantern into the vertical position**

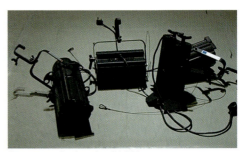

Lanterns before! – GMSL

Step 3
- ✓ **Release the safety bond** from the bar, coil it up and attach to the lantern
- ✓ **Slacken the wing bolt** on the hanging clamp
- ✓ **Lift the lantern off the bar** with the hanging clamp attached and place it lens down on the floor

If you have followed the above instructions:
- ✓ **The lanterns should stand vertically** on its colour runners without falling over
- ✓ **The shutters and barndoors will be protected** and they will not become damaged or bent
- ✓ **The cables and safety bonds will not be trailing on the floor** when the lantern is moved

Lanterns afterwards – GMSL

De-rigging accessories

☑ Remove the filter from the colour frame and store in a colour storage folder

☑ Store the barndoors and colour frames in an accessories tray

➤ Coiling up extension cables

There is a simple and effective way to coil cables. If you are right-handed:

1 Hold the socket end of the cable in the left hand (or the right hand if you are left-handed)
2 Allow the cable to run through the fingers of the right hand (or vice versa)
3 Extend the right arm out to measure a standard length for the loop
4 As the first loop is made, twist the cable with the right fingers to remove any kinks

Coiling a cable – GMSL

5 Repeat measuring the length of cable for the next loop, twisting to remove the kinks
6 The loops of the coil should now all be the same length hanging free without any twist or kinks
7 Tape the coil together with PVC tape or use tie lines; see 'How they do it in North America'

➤ Organising accessories

Plastic tool trays provide a quick, convenient and portable storage for colour frames, barndoors and spare lamps. They can be lifted out and used on-stage as the accessories are de-rigged, preventing them from being left lying around becoming lost or damaged.

Extension cables – sort into standard lengths, 5m, 10m and 20m and colour code by attaching a small band of PVC tape at both ends to help identify them by their length. Store the cables by their sizes in large plastic boxes or crates marked with the length and colour.

How they do it in North America

Using PVC tape to hold a coil of cable together is considered very bad practice in USA:

'This is bad working practice in North America. As with securing cable to bars, we use "tie line," what would be called "sash" or "sash cord" in the UK. It is the sign of a well-organized and well-maintained theatre to have a piece of tie line attached to the male end of a cable with an overhand knot with long tails extending; that way, when you coil the

3 WORKING WITH LANTERNS | **A quick start**

cable, you tie the ends in a BOW (always a bow!) around the entire coil, making for easy undoing, no wasted or messy tape on the floor, and no adhesive sticking to the cable! The same is done to secure a cable to a bar, as it allows for more movement slack if pulled, less mess and less waste of tape since the lengths are reusable, and ease of removal from the bar (just pull the end of the bow!).'[10]

Perhaps we should consider adopting this as good working practice in the UK? It would certainly save a lot of waste and could be a green issue.

Cable connectors

Each country use different types of cable plugs and sockets; they can have 2 or 3 pins that are round, flat and parallel or angled.

The size of the connectors and diameter of the pins depends upon the maximum power handling of the cable being used that is measured in amps. See Part 3: 'Lighting Resources – Technical info.'.

➢ **In the UK:**

- **15 amp round 3 pin** outlet plugs and sockets are used in the UK on dimmer packs, cable patches and in most lighting installations to provide power from a dimmer. Therefore the cable from a generic or conventional lantern is terminated in a 15 amp plug top.
- **CEE P17 3 pin** cable plugs and sockets are used in the UK for mains power connections; 16A, 32A, 63A and 125 amp for power distribution and dimmer pack connections.
- **CEE P17 3 pin 16 amp** outlet plugs and sockets are used mainly in the UK to provide 'hot power' for fixtures that require a non-dim circuit supply. Moving heads, LED luminaires, colour scrollers and discharge lamp fixtures. These fixtures require direct power and will be damaged if connected to a dimmer controlled circuit.[11] In the UK these fixtures are normally terminated in 16 amp CEE P17 cable plugs so as to distinguish their connection from generic lanterns requiring a dimmer circuit.

15 Amp outlet socket – GMSL

16A CEE P17 connector – Stage Electrics

[10] Ziggy Jacobs – an American Lighting Design student, Central School of Speech and Drama
[11] See Chapter 6 'DMX Fixtures – A quick start' – Animated and intelligent fixtures

However it must not be assumed that 16 amp CEE P17 sockets to be the norm for only non-dim circuits as dimmer packs are available with CEE P17 16 amp outlet sockets as an alternative to the round pin15 amp sockets. CEE P17 connectors are also used for outdoor temporary installations as they provide a good waterproof connection and are occasionally used in some installations for the termination of the outgoing dimmer controlled circuits.

Therefore it is important when working with fixtures that require a non-dim circuit to verify that the CEE P1716 amp sockets are clearly marked as 'hot power' and that they are not controlled by a dimmer before powering up non dim fixtures.[12]

Lantern reference guide

To find the wattage, type of lamp and the size of colour frame, gobo holders and gobos for each make and type of lantern – see Part 3: 'Lighting Resources – Technical info.'.

GLOBAL JARGON

- **Lighting bar** (UK) – **'Pipe'** 1¼ OD outside diameter commonly called **'Batten'** (NA)
- **IWB** – Internally Wired Bar (UK) – **'Batten'** fed by with power **'electric'** (NA)
- **Hanging clamps** (UK & Europe) – are used to hang lanterns on lighting bars
- **Pipe or C-clamps** (NA) – are used to hang lanterns on pipes
- **Hanging clamps & light weight half couplers** (NZ & Aus) – are used to hang lanterns on **'spot bars'** (NZ) and **'pipes'** (Aus)
- **Safety bond** (UK) – **'safety wire'**, **'safety chain'** or **'safety cables'** (NA)
- **Plugs & Sockets** (UK) – 'male end' – **'Plug'** and 'female end' – **'Receptacle'** (NA)
- **Flexible cable** mains lead (UK) – **'Cord'** or **'Power cable'** (NA)
- **Borderlights** or **Strips** (NA) mulit-lamp, compartmented lighting luminaires used for wash lighting – **'Flood Battens'** Strand Coda 4

---

[12] See Chapter 4 'Dimmers – More info' – Distributed power control systems

Did you know that –

■ Electric compartment battens were first hung on the 2" gas barrels that supplied the original gas lighting, hence the term 'pipe' used in some countries for lighting bars. The electric battens were replaced by floods and spotlights.

■ Compartment battens were used to provide over stage lighting and to light backcloths and skycloths. They consisted of a series of tungsten domestic type bulbs called after their rounded shape, each having a reflector mounted in a separate metal compartment with a colour frame. The batten was usually wired in four consecutive circuits to provide Red, Green, Blue and White light. The battens would be linked together to cover the full width of the stage. Footlight battens were recessed in the front of the stage to remove the shadows cast by the overhead lighting. Groundrow battens were used at floor level to light the bottom of a skycloth or cyclorama"

■ In North America lighting bars are called 'battens' which presumably dates back to the time when overhead stage lighting was provide by the compartment battens of electric light.

■ The 48mm diameter is now the standard size for stage lighting bars in the UK which is the same size as aluminium scaffolding bars

■ In 1959, the 'hook clamp' was introduced by Strand Electric, having a finger-tightened wing set screw. This revolutionised the rigging of lanterns, replacing the original 'L'-shaped bracket and bolted pipe clip requiring the use of a spanner

■ Philips Selecon have added a number of design safety features to their lanterns, including a retractable safety wire and flip-top colour runner boxes, taking lantern design into the 21st century

■ **15 amp plugs and sockets** were originally used for domestic power sockets in the UK prior to the introduction of 13 amp ring circuit/mains and the use of fused plug tops

■ **Flat pinned 13 amp connectors** are not used in the UK for stage lighting installations because the plug tops contain a fuse. The circuit protection on stage lighting is provided at the source by a circuit breaker or fuse on the dimmer unit. Therefore, additional fuse protection is unnecessary and would cause confusion in location faults

QUICK TIPS

- Before hanging a lantern, make sure that the stirrup/hanging bracket is in direct line with the axis of the lantern so that it will hang in a vertical position when hung on the bar
- Base down mounted lamps are designed to be burnt at an optimum angle of 45 degrees either side of the vertical
- If the lantern is hung upside down or at a side angle, it will greatly reduce the life of the lamp
- Axial lanterns, Parcans and Floods can be used in a vertical position without reducing the lamp life
- Check that the lantern is hanging or mounted the right way up with the cable entry at the bottom
- When mounting a lantern on a stand, remember to reverse the position of the stirrup if it has been hanging to ensure that it is the right way up
- When removing a lantern from a stand, reverse the stirrup before hanging it on a bar
- Save your lamps! Don't use lanterns as working lights
- Domestic linear lamp Flood lights make good working lights
- Tool trays can be purchased from DIY stores
- It is easier to identify the length of extension cables if they are colour coded
- De-rigging cables from a lighting bar – always start from the end with the shortest cables to save ending up with a knot of cables like a pile of spaghetti
- Cables have a mind of their own! Never coil them on your arm round your hand and elbow because the twists will be left in the cable and the coil will not stay together

Points for action

Takes longer

- Check that you have frames to fit all the different sizes of the models of lanterns and replace them where necessary

A proper job!

- Organise the colour frames and barndoors into tool trays and mark them with large labels
- Large labels can be produced on a computer; print and laminate them, and attach them with double-sided adhesive tape
- Colour code extension cables, e.g. 5M – Brown, 10M – Orange, 20M – Green

More info – Lantern maintenance

A lot of time can be wasted when focusing dirty lanterns or faulty equipment with missing parts. Preparing the equipment can save a lot of valuable time when you are lighting the show.

Maintaining lanterns

➤ Cleaning

Lanterns need to be cleaned at least once a year. A build up of dust on the lens can considerably reduce the intensity of the lamp and it can be a safety hazard. Remove the dust from the lens, reflector, inner and outer casing of the lantern with paintbrush and cloth; a face mask should be worn to provide protection.

➤ Friction hanging bolt suspension

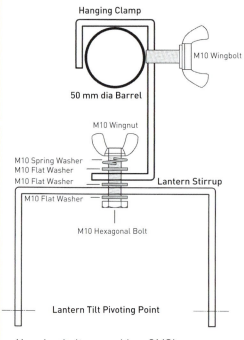

Hanging bolt assembly – GMSL

Tightening the assembly – GMSL

A friction hanging bolt assembly saves a lot of time when angling and focusing lanterns as it allows the lantern to be rotated but holds it firmly in position after it has been adjusted. The assembly consists of a series of flat washers between each moving surface to allow the parts to rotate under the pressure of a spring washer that maintains the tension and prevents any additional movement. The friction assembly removes the need to use a spanner every time a lantern is repositioned.

➤ **Attaching safety bonds/chains**

Attaching a safety bond – GMSL

The safety bond/wire is a load tested steel cable with a loop at one end and a clip at the other.

- The safety bond should be permanently attached to the lantern to stop it falling to the floor when the lantern is being struck
- On lanterns with anchor points, pass the loop at the end of the cable through the hole, thread the hook end of the cable through the loop and pull tight
- Safety bonds in the UK are marked with the safe working load
- Check that you are using the correct size safety bond to match the weight of the lantern

Troubleshooting

➤ **If a lantern isn't working:**

1 **Isolate the lantern** – switch off the main electrical power supply as there might be an electrical fault and the lantern could be live

2 **Check the Miniature Circuit breaker trip switch** (MCB) or fuse on the dimmer unit control[13]

3 **If the MCB is in the on position** or the fuse intact, check the circuit and cabling by substituting a known working lantern and test the circuit

4 **If the MCB has tripped out** or the fuse is blown, this would indicate that there is an electrical fault or that the lamp has blown

5 **Allow the lantern to cool down** before touching it

6 **Disconnect the lantern**

7 **Strike the lantern** – it is always safer to work on it at floor level

8 **Inspect the lantern** for any obvious visual electrical faults in the wiring. If in doubt, remove the lantern from service and refer it to a qualified electrician

9 **Inspect the lamp** – if the filament is intact, there could be an electrical fault and remove the lantern from service

10 **If the filament is broken**, replace the lamp

[13] Dimmer units, MCBs and fuse circuit protection, see Chapter 4 'Dimmers – More info'

3 WORKING WITH LANTERNS

More info

11 Test the lantern by using a known working circuit outlet socket on a dimmer rack. If the lantern still doesn't work, there must be an electrical fault

↓

12 If it works, hang the lantern and reconnect to the original circuit and test

Replacing lamps

➤ **The lamp housing**

- On a Profile lantern, the lamp housing is at the rear with the access either from the side or underneath the housing
- On an Axial Ellipsoidal lantern, the lamp is positioned on the end of the lantern
- On Fresnels and PCs, the front of the lantern hinges forward or access may be from the side

➤ **Three types of lamp bases used in lanterns**

- **Bipost base lamps** as used on modern lanterns have a two pin base. To remove, gently ease out or use the release lever on Selecon lanterns to part eject the lamp
- **Prefocus cap lamps** as used on older lanterns are held in place by two fins that line up the filament of the lamp in the lamp post holder so that it is at 90° to the axis of the lantern. To remove, press the lamp down against the strung base and turn anticlockwise through 90 degrees
- **'K' class linear lamps** as used in Cyc and Floods have terminals at either end of the tube and fit into a sprung lamp post holder
- **When handling tungsten halogen lamps**, always use protective gloves or a soft cloth as grease from your fingers burns on to and through the glass envelope that will affect the halogen cycle and shorten the life of the lamp[14]

Bipost base CP class 'compact filament' lamp – GMSL

☑ **Check the lamp**
- **Check to see if the filament is broken** by holding the lamp up to the light
- **Check to see if there are any dark finger-shaped burns** on the glass envelope from where it has been previously touched which will have reduced the life of the lamp
- **Check the pins on the base of the lamp** to see if there is any sign of burning from arcing caused by poor contacts and a faulty lamp post holder that may need to be replaced
- **If there is no obvious fault**, it could be an electrical fault in the lantern's wiring

[14] *A Beginner's Guide to Stage Lighting*, Peter Coleman

3 WORKING WITH LANTERNS   More info

✓ **Check the type of lamp and wattage**

Most commonly used lamps:

T18	T26	T11	T29	GKV600	HPL575	HPL750
500 watt	650 watt	1000 watt	1200 watt	600 watt	575 watt	750 watt
Focus lanterns CCT, Philips Selecon & Strand				**Axial lanterns** Acclaim, SPX, Pacific, SL	**Axial lanterns** Source Four	

Lanterns Reference Guide data sheet – Check out Part 3: Lighting Resources – Technical Info

Fitting a new lamp
- **Clean the lens** and reflector before fitting a new lamp
- **Remove the lamp** from the top of the box and hold it by its metal base below the glass envelope
- **Use a soft cloth** or gloves when handling the lamp
- **Bipost lamps** – line up the large and small pin with the base of the lamp post holder and firmly push home
- **Prefocus lamps** – line up the large and small fins with the openings on the base of the lamp post holder, press down and turn clockwise through 90 degrees

Test the lantern, close the lantern housing and test it on a known working dimmer channel. If possible, always protect theatre lamps by using a dimmer control as a sudden electrical surge from a switched supply can cause the filament to blow which can be an expensive mistake

LAMPS NOT BULBS!

It is important to use the correct terms –
'The lamp produces the light in a lantern; we plant bulbs in the garden!' [15/16]

And as they say in North America:
Q: 'How many techies does it take to change a light bulb?'
A: 'We don't, it's called a lamp, you idiot!' [17]

[15] *A Beginner's Guide to Stage Lighting*, Peter Coleman
[16] 'A Glossary of Technical Terms', www.theatrecrafts.com/glossary
[17] Ziggy Jacobs – American Lighting Design student

3 WORKING WITH LANTERNS | More info

Types of lamps

There are three types of lamp sources that are used in theatre lanterns – Incandescent, Discharge and LED.

➤ **Incandescent lamps**
- **Tungsten-halogen lamps** have a tungsten wire filament enclosed in a halogen-filled glass envelope
- **As used in** theatre generic lanterns, some moving lights, also for TV and film lanterns

Types of incandescent lamps

Class	Colour Temperature	Use
T Class	3000 degrees Kelvin	Stage lighting
CP Class	3200 degrees Kelvin – slightly higher	Originally used for television and film
HPL & GKV	3000 degrees Kelvin	Ellipsoidal/Axial lanterns
K Class	lower colour temp than T or CP Class lamps	Floodlights – linear double-ended lamps
ANSI Lamps		PAR fittings – sealed beam lamps

➤ **Discharge lamps**
- **Metal-halide lamps** have two metal rods separated by a small gap enclosed in a gas-filled glass envelope; the high voltage passed between the electrodes causes the gas to conduct electricity. Discharge lamps emit a higher light output and have a longer life than incandescent lamps. Discharge lamps cannot be dimmed so the lanterns are fitted with shutters to control the intensity of the light. Some discharge lamps do not have the facility for 'hot restrike' and may require up to 15–20 minutes to cool down before they can be restruck again
- **Colour temperature** of a discharge lamp is significantly bluer than the white of a tungsten-halogen lamp. This can cause problems in using and blending generic lanterns with moving lights, although this is not so much a problem with follow spots
- **As used in** moving lights, follow spots, effects projectors, also for TV and film and generic lanterns used for display and exhibitions

Types of discharge lamps

CSI	CDM	HMI	MSR
Compact Source Iodide, 5520 K	Ceramic Discharge Metal-halide, 4200 K	Halide Metal Iodide, 5600 K	Medium Source Rare-earth, 5600 K
Follow spots	**Display fittings**	**Moving lights**	**Moving lights, follow spots**

➤ **LED light sources**
LED light sources are at the time of writing in a continual state of development by a number of lighting manufacturers. There is no common standard and the different arrays of LEDs that are used depends upon the individual manufacturers preference. Therefore there are a number of variations used to produce white light and accurate colour mixing.

- **White light**: WW, NW, CW, TW/VW
  Warm 3000 K, Tungsten 3200 K, Neutral 4000K, Cool 5600 K, colour temperatures, Tunable or Variable Whites
- **Saturated colours & pastel tints**: RGB+W, RGB+A
  The colours are produced by mixing an arrays Red, Green, Blue + White, or + Amber LED emitters
- **7 Colour System**: RGB+4
  Four additional LED emitters, greens, mid blues and ambers are added to Red, Green, Blue emitters to produce a good white and a smoother and more subtle range of tints and deeper, richer colours

➤ **Colour temperature**: The source of light from the three types of lamps has a different colour temperature that is measured in degrees Kelvin K, as can be seen below. It can be difficult to blend the colour temperature from the different light sources in a lighting rig or they may be used in contrast to produce an effect.

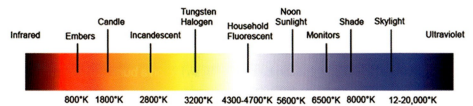

Sources of light color temperatures – Thomas Nell, 'Spotlight'[18]

---

[18] 'All the world is a stage' seminar notes Thomas Nell, 'Spotlight'

3 WORKING WITH LANTERNS   More info

Extras! – Electrical safety

It is important to personally check all equipment, lanterns and cables that they are electrically safe to use before using them

'The trouble about electricity is that it gives no warning of its dangers. It is a quiet, unseen, obedient servant who at any time, given the chance, will round on his employer and may even slay him!'

Frederick Bentham, The Art of Stage Lighting

Electrical testing

The line manager of the theatre or studio space is responsible for ensuring the electrical safety of the installation and equipment. In the UK, regular inspection and testing of the fixed installation and the portable electrical equipment is required to satisfy the 'Electricity at Work Regulations' 1989.

➤ **The Institution of Electrical Engineers (UK) (IEE) – Code of Practice**[19] states that every installation requires regular inspection which for theatre spaces should consist of:

- **A periodic electrical test** of the lighting bars, wiring installation, dimmers and control
- **P**ortable **A**ppliance **T**esting, **PAT testing** – theatrical equipment should be inspected and tested by a competent and trained electrician; each item should be marked with the test date sticker, a record of testing and repairs should be kept

➤ **The IEE 'Electrical Maintenance including Portable Appliance Testing'**[20] **recommends:**
The testing of fixed electrical installations – a maximum period between inspections of:

- **Theatres**   1 year
- **Educational establishments**   5 years
- **Emergency lighting**   3 years

Moveable, portable and hand-held equipment that is in regular use – the following good working practice should be carried out:

- **User visual checks**   Weekly
- **Formal visual inspection**   4 months
- **Inspection and testing**   12 months

[19] The Institution of Electrical Engineers 'Code of Practice for In-Service Inspection and Testing of Electrical Equipment'
[20] The Institution of Electrical Engineers 'Electrical Maintenance including Portable Appliance Testing'

Checking electrical equipment

Making a formal visual inspection – every 4 months

➤ **Disconnect the equipment before inspecting and check for the following faults:**

✓ **Flexible cables** – cuts in the outer insulation cable or damage covered by tape. The size of cable is suitable for the intended load, 2.5mm TRS should be used with 15/16 amp cable plugs and sockets

Damaged cable – GMSL

✓ **Flexible plug top & cable socket/connectors** – outer covering of the flexible cable is firmly held at the point of entry by the cable grip and that the plug top hasn't been cut, damaged or that there are signs of overheating caused by loose internal connections

Damaged plug top – GMSL

✓ **Wiring of connectors** – check that the live, neutral and earth cables are connected to the correct terminal pins, that the internal wires are fully insulated and are not too long, the terminal screws and outer cable grip screws are tight and that the live and neutral sprung terminal shutters are in place

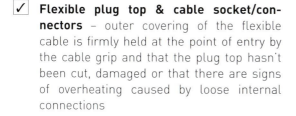

Correctly wired – GMSL

✓ **NB** The rewiring of flexible cable plugs and sockets/connectors should only be carried out by a competent electrician

✓ **Lanterns** – outer covering of flexible cable firmly held at the point of entry, a fault found on older lanterns

✓ **Old lanterns** – secondary earth bonding between the moving parts can be found on all new lanterns. It is wise to check that older lanterns have been updated to meet the current requirements and that there is earth bonding from the lamp tray to the outer body and to the hinged sides or fronts

Lantern cable entry – GMSL

➤ **Flexible power 3 core cable – colour coding**

Country	UK/EU – IEC	Australia/NZ/ South Africa	US/Canada
(L) Single phase Live/hot	Brown	Red, Brown	Black
(N) Neutral/cold	Blue	Black, Blue	White
(PE) Protective earth/ground	Green/yellow (bi-colour)	Green, Green/yellow	Green

IEC – International Electrotechnical Commission

➤ **If you find an electrical fault**
- **Switch off – do not use the equipment**
- **Disconnect**/unplug it from the mains supply
- **Remove it from use** and immediately report it to the technical manager or chief electrician
- **Label the equipment – 'Electrical fault: do not use'**

Did you know that –
- Flexible cables in the UK pre-1977 were colour coded, Live – red, Neutral – black, Earth – green
- Non-flexible cables in the UK finally changed to the IEC harmonised colours in 1999 in line with the EU

GLOBAL JARGON
- **Single phase Live** (UK) – **Hot** or **Live** (NA), **Active** (Aus)
- **Neutral** (UK) – **Cold** (NA)
- **Protective earth** (UK) – **Ground** or **Grounding conductor** (NA)

EXTRA TIPS

■ Regular user checks are vital for electrical safety

■ On the annual PAT test, the equipment is most likely to fail on the visual inspection even before it is electrically tested for insulation and earth continuity

■ 13 amp plug tops on non-lighting equipment should have sleeved live and negative pins

■ It is also good practice to use sleeved 15 amp plug tops

■ TRS Tough Rubber Sheaved is preferred to PVC for flexible cables as it has increased flexibility, easier to coil free from twists and kinks

■ Use heavier-duty extension cables on extra-long runs to prevent a voltage drop

■ Avoid having thick bunches of cables or coils of cable as they can overheat

Extra resources – go to

www.pat-testing.info – Information on PAT testing, good example of how to wire a connector/plug

Points for action

Quickies!

■ Make a visual inspection of a lantern and cable to check for electrical faults

■ When were they last PAT tested?

Takes longer

■ Check out the dates and records of when the lanterns and cables were last tested

■ Carry out a visual inspection of a cable plug or socket and check the connections

3 WORKING WITH LANTERNS

Extras!

5 Lighting control

A quick start – Manual lighting control desks

Looking at the functions and ways of operating a manual lighting control desk

More info – Memory lighting control desks

Looking at the functions and ways of operating a memory lighting control desk

Extras! – DMX Digital multiplexing

An introduction to the DMX 512 control system

A quick start – Manual lighting control desks

The lighting control desk is the centre of the stage lighting system. Understanding the function of the manual lighting desk provides the basis of knowledge and understanding for moving on to memory control desks.

Manual lighting control desks

➤ **Manual desks consist of:**

- **Channel faders** which control the level of the dimmer unit and the light produced by the lantern. The fader has a graduated scale; as it is raised from 0 to 10 the light increases and from 10 to 0 the brightness decreases. This is called the 'Raise' and 'Fade'

ETC Smart Fade 12 – ETC

- **Scene presets** – there are two banks of independently controlled channel faders. Each scene preset can be used independently to set up a separate scene or picture of light that can be saved as a written plot or saved in the lighting desk memory as a lighting cue
- **Preset Masters** – each preset has a master fader that controls the maximum output levels of the channel faders allowing two scenes of lighting to be set up and crossfaded from one to the other

- **Control desks** which are powered by a local mains power socket that needs to be switched on before it can be used. Some analogue desks are powered directly from the dimmer packs

➢ **Overview of a 12-way 2 preset control desk**

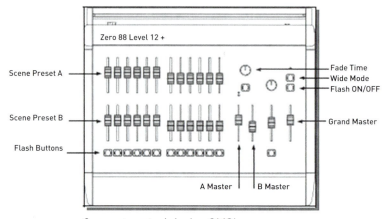

2 preset control desk – GMSL

- **Scene Preset A** – 12 channel faders controlling the output levels of the dimmer channels
- **Scene Preset B** – 12 duplicate channel faders controlling the same dimmer channels
- **Channel faders** – numbered 1–6, 7–12, are each graduated with a scale of 1–10
- **Master A** – controls the maximum output levels of the Scene Preset A channel faders
- **Master B** – controls the maximum output levels of the Scene Preset B channel faders
- **Grand Master** – controls the maximum output levels of all channels on both presets and channel flash buttons
- **Crossfading** – Master A scale works from 10 to 0 top to bottom
    Master B scale is reversed 0 to 10 top to bottom
    When the master faders are moved together in tandem:
    Master A fades down from 10 to 0 and Master B rises from 0 to 10
- **'Dipless' crossfade** – channels having the same intensity on both presets will stay at a constant level of intensity
- **Fade time control** – sets the time taken to crossfade between the two scene presets
- **'BO'** – Black Out button overrides the master faders switching everything off

Side tab: A quick start   5 LIGHTING CONTROL

- **Channel flash buttons** – flashes the channels to the level set on the Grand Master
- **Wide mode** – 12/24 control desk can be used as a 12-way 2 preset or set in wide mode to a 24-way single preset control desk; the preset B faders are marked with dual numbers 1/13, 2/14–12/24
- **Sequence effects memory** – basic memory feature to program and play back a chase of repeated sequences of patterns or flashing lights
- **Basic memory functions** – on some manual desks, it is possible to record and play back a limited number of sequence effects or stacks of scenes of light/lighting cues

> **Online video link – 5.1: Manual control desks**
> https://vimeo.com/123717494

Using a two scene preset control desk

➤ **Setting the lighting scenes:**
- **Masters A & B** – set Preset Master A to level '10' and Preset Master B to level '0'
- **Live preset A** – set the circuit fader levels for the first scene of light (Cue 1)
- **Crossfade Masters A & B** – Master A to level '0' and Master B to level '10'
- **Live preset B** – set the circuit fader levels for the second scene of light (Cue 2)
- **Crossfade Masters A & B** – Master A to '10' and Master B to '0'
- **Live preset A** – set the circuit faders for the third scene of light (Cue 3)

A written plot will need to be made of the channel fader levels on the preset for each lighting cue

➤ **Running the lighting scenes:**
When the master fader is at '0', the preset it controls is 'Dead' and the channel faders can be set without affecting the levels of light on the 'Live' preset.

- **Masters A & B** – set to level '0'
- **Preset A 'Dead'** – preset the circuit fader levels for Cue 1
- **Master A** – Cue 1, raise to level '10', preset A 'Live'
- **Preset B 'Dead'** – preset the circuit fader levels for Cue 2
- **Crossfade Masters** – Master A – '0', Master B – '10', preset B 'Live'
- **Preset A 'Dead'** – preset the circuit faders for Cue 3
- **Crossfade Masters** – Master A – '10', Master B – '0', preset A 'Live'
- **Crossfade times** – can be done manually or preset using the fade time control. Set the control to the required time sequence and activate on cue by quickly moving the master faders together. The fade time control can be adjusted to override the time during the cue to speed it up or slow it down

5 LIGHTING CONTROL   **A quick start**

QUICK TIPS

- ■ When flashing through lanterns, set the Grand Master at a lower level to protect the filament in the lamps
- ■ If the control desk isn't working, check the blackout switch is off and the preset and Grand Master is at level 10
- ■ If the masters don't appear to work on a crossfade, check that the fade time control is set to manual and not 5 minutes!
- ■ To override a live timed fade, turn the speed control to speed up or slow down

Points for action

Quickies!

- ■ Check out your lighting control desk and see what facilities are available

Takes longer

- ■ Set up a lighting scene on both presets and use the manual crossfade
- ■ Use the fade time control and see the effect of various lengths of time

More info – Memory lighting control desks

With the developments in technology, many features that were originally provided in the advanced memory controls can now be found on the basic memory lighting desks. Some have the provision to control a small number of moving lights.

Memory control desks

Memory control desks have a built-in specialist computer that can save and play back all the information for the lighting of a show. Lighting scenes can be preprogrammed and played back with timed crossfades.

Three types of memory functions:
- **Scene memory stack** – 'scenes' or 'states' of lighting are set up on a scene preset and saved as cues in a numerical sequence as used for a conventional drama production
- **Sequence memory** – recording a sequence of running 'steps' or changes of individual levels of light from lanterns used to produce a 'chase' or flashing effects as used to create special effects as in pop concerts
- **Sub-masters** – assigning scenes or states of lighting to a dedicated channel fader/sub-master. This is particularly useful where there are natural sequences and repeated states of lighting as used in concerts, pop music events or dance shows. The desired scene of lighting can instantaneously be recalled by raising the sub-master fader, allowing the operator to 'busk' the show and to make a more spontaneous response for live shows

> **Online video link – 5.2: Memory Control Desks**
> https://vimeo.com/123717495

Basic memory lighting control desk

Memory control desks have a number of common features; however, there can be variations depending upon the make and model. The basic memory desk has a similar layout to the manual desk but has additional sections for memory, control and other functions.

Jester desk – Zero 88, Eaton's Cooper Control

➤ **Generic lighting controls**
- **Channel control faders** – 12 or 24 channels on two scene presets or in wide mode 24 or 48 single channel control faders
- **Sub-masters** – Scene preset B channel faders can be selected to double up as sub-masters. The sub-masters can be increased by selecting memory pages, e.g.

2 pages x 12 channels = 24 sub-masters, 2 pages x 24 channels = 48 sub-masters

- **Masters** –
  Preset Masters A & B controlling the maximum level of output from the individual preset channel faders and crossfading facility
  Grand Master controlling the maximum output level of the flash buttons on both presets

➤ **Memory controls**

Jester program mode – Zero 88, Eaton's Cooper Control

- **Program mode** – selecting scene memory, sequence memory, sub-master memory
- **Sequence/chase control** – run modes
  Direction:
  - Forwards
  - Backwards
  - Auto reverse
  - Random
  Attack:
  - Snap on/Snap off
  - Snap on/Fade off
  - Fade on/Snap off
  - Fade on/Fade off

- **Editing** – clear, reset, cut & paste
- **Page selection** – A & B, 12 x 2 pages of memory 24 scenes, 24 x 2 pages memory 48 scenes
- **Store/program**

➤ **Play back**
- **'Go'/'pause'** button
- **Fade time** control
- **Memory master** controlling the overall level of memory output
- **Sequence speed** control
- **Auxiliary buttons** – triggering simple DMX controlled devices, scrollers, smoke machines and strobes

➤ **Screens, monitors & storage**
- **LCD desk screen** – small screen displaying basic functions and information on cues
- **External monitor** – displaying the output levels and memory information
- **USB storage** – USB port to back up the show on an external memory device

Advanced memory control desks

Advanced memory control desks have a larger number of control channels than the basic memory lighting control and an advanced memory effects engine that provides additional control for moving lights, LED fixtures, scrollers and effects, smoke, mist machines and strobe lighting. They are mainly used for structured programming and playback as used for theatre productions.

➤ **The DMX control channels are assigned to:**
- Manually operated channel faders controlling dimmer units and the generic lanterns
- The attributes/functions of automated fixtures, moving lights, LED fixtures, scrollers, mist machines and other effects

➤ **DMX controls for moving lights/fixtures**
Fixture attribute/selection buttons
- Intensity/brightness
- Colour
- Beam shape – pattern/gobo
- Position

Solution – Zero 88, Eaton's Cooper Control

➤ **Control wheels assigned to fixture personality**
- Brightness – 0–100%
- Colour – Cyan, Magenta, Yellow
- Pattern – gobo wheel 1, gobo wheel 2, Prism, prism rotation, speed
- Beam shape – shutter, focus
- Position – pan, tilt, speed

Solution control wheels – Zero 88, Cooper Control

➤ **Other features**
- Additional pages of memory increase the size of the scene memory stack, number of sequences and sub-master states that can be saved
- External desk monitors to preview, edit scenes and plot 'blind' cues on the monitor using the desk without the dimmers or lanterns being connected
- Fixture libraries provide the facility to select the preprogrammed attributes/ personalities of all the standard DMX fixtures when setting up the fixtures control
- Colour picking – colour pallets provide an approximate selection from the standard ranges of colour filters to be reproduced by DMX controlled fixtures. The pre-loaded colour pallets of the Apollo, GAM, Lee & Rosco ranges of colour filters can be selected by make and number, e.g. Lee 106 or on screen colour display
- LED colour picking – The ETC Source Four LED 2 luminaire provides a dead on colour match to standard colour filters when used with the colour library that is built into the ETC Eos control desk

5 LIGHTING CONTROL   More info

■ Effects engines provide preprogrammed effects that can be used with all fixtures/attributes, Fly Ins, Can Cans, Rainbows and Iris Pulses[27]

More advanced lighting desks

Advanced lighting desks have been developed to control the increased number of DMX control channels and Universes for scrollers, moving heads, LED fixtures, effects, digital projection and pixel mapping now being used in theatres and for events. They have also been developed for specific user requirements within the entertainment industry;

Eos Ti control desk – ETC

■ **Integrated desks** as used in theatres for drama and musical theatre
■ **Live desks** for concerts and events
■ **Crossover desks** merging the features of both integrated and live desks for the mixed requirements of epic theatre, television and award events.

Integrated lighting desks

Integrated lighting desks provide for the more structured approach of lighting as used for drama, musicals and dance. The control channels can be assigned to a reduced number of channels and group faders by using a numeric key pad or touch screen to input the control data that is displayed on the monitor screens. On the high-end desks 'Magic Sheets' can be programmed to show on a monitor the diagrammatic layout of the lanterns and fixtures in the rig showing that are being used for easy reference and selection.

Magic Sheet – ETC

ETC 'Eos' and 'Ion' integrated lighting desks and Phillips Strand 500 series are commonly used on Broadway and for West End shows. They are also a standard in most receiving theatres in the UK. The following control desks are currently being used in the West End:

ETC Eos: *'Titanium Ti'*, *'Shakespeare in Love'*, *'Jeeves and Wooster'*, *'Dirty Dancing'*, *'Dirty Rotten Scoundrels'*, *'Les Miserables'*, *'Billy Elliot'*. **Strand 502i** *'Phantom of the Opera"* where as **ETC Ion** was used for the 2012 tour of *'Phantom'*.

---

[27] Zero 88 Product Guide – Leap Frog

Live lighting desks

Live lighting desks are designed for fast, intuitive hands-on control of large numbers of moving lights, generic lanterns and LED fixtures that can be found in festival, concerts and arena events. Touch screens facilitate ultrafast programming and the provision of motorized master faders provide smooth operation or automatic playback for 'busking the show' that is often required on live gigs and concert tours. Most common desks used are from Avolites, High End Systems and ChamSys.

Hog 4 – High End Systems

Sapphire Touch – Avolites

Crossover lighting desks

Crossover lighting desks combine the features found in integrated and live desks. The use of touch screens provide an interactive control to create groups, palettes and presets as building blocks for the show and to configure effects playback combining generics, moving heads, LED fixtures and media servers. They are highly suited for the mix of structured and unstructured playback using master playbacks and motorized faders. This provides the programmer

Grand MA2 – MA Lighting

with the flexibility to customize the desk to control the lighting and effects for the event or show to their personal requirements. Many of the desks have the provision of integrated keyboard to input information on cues and notes.

Crossover desks have become a standard choice for musical theatre in the West End:
grand MA2: 'Book of Mormon', 'Charlie and the Chocolate Factory', 'Matilda', 'Wicked' and 'Shrek the Musical' tour. Also as used at 'Royal Shakespeare Theatre' Stratford-upon-Avon, 'Metropolitan Opera House'' New York. This possibly reflects the increasing demands of their productions.

5 LIGHTING CONTROL

More info

Crossover lighting desks

➤ **Phillips Strand 'Neo'**:

*"**Seize the light**; to grab, move, change position, color and motivate the lighting design simply and effectively."*[28]

➤ **ETC 'Cobalt'**:

*"**Touch the Light** – What if you could reach out and touch the light – craft it, color it, move it – directly and without feeling like there's a machine between you and your design? You see the light in your head and with minimal keystrokes see that creation on stage. Cobalt™ is designed from the ground up to get you from thought to reality as quickly as possible. Short commands coupled with direct-access touch screen tools make the console disappear under your fingertips – nothing stands between you and the light."*

See www.etcconnect.com/products – What's happening at ETC – 'Are you ready for Cobalt tm?'

Cobalt control desk – ETC

The Future may well be different with the further development of hybrid crossover desks combining the best of and merging the integrated and live control desks. The ultimate choice especially for the theatre may eventually be over which manufactures platform to adopt, rather than a particular control desk. However there will always be the stand alone desks, Avolites and High End Systems that remain the standard choice for the big musical concert events.

Lighting control desks makes & models

See Part 3 Lighting Resources – 'Technical info'

---

[28] www.strandlighting.com /Consoles/Neo lighting console

5 LIGHTING CONTROL   More info

Did you know that -

■ In 1933, General Electrics Radio City Music Hall, New York was one of the first to have multi-scene preset controls and to be mounted in front of the stage

■ In 1949, Strand Electrics Light Console was based on the design of an organ console and it was the first lighting control desk to be mounted in a front of house position at the London Palladium theatre

■ In the 1960s, preset control desks were developed using the thyristor electronic dimmer

■ Prior to memory controls being available, three scene presets were developed to manage the longer setting-up time from a manual plot where there were a large number of faders being used

■ 'Strand Three Set' had three presets and each preset had three group masters. Individual channel faders could be assigned to and controlled by a group master within the preset

■ 'Board Op' and 'On the Board' are terms still used from the days when there were resistance dimmer control boards

Extra resources — go to

www.avolites.org.uk –	Avolites
www.adblighting.com –	ADB Lighting Technologies
www.chamsys.co.uk –	ChamSys
www.etcconnect.com –	ETC
www.highend.com	High End Systems
www.jands.com –	Jands Pty Ltd
www.lsclighting.com –	LSC Lighting Systems
www.malighting.de –	MA Lighting International
www.strandlighting.com –	Philips Strand Lighting
www.Zero88.com –	Zero.88

5 LIGHTING CONTROL

More info

➤ **Inner workings of a moving head fixture**

The cutaway section of XR 1000 Spot shows all the inner working parts that produces the effects projected by an animated Spot moving head.

Cutaway of XR 1000 Spot – PR Lighting

Automated lighting rigs

In many of the larger theatres moving heads are included in the permanent lighting rig to meet the demands of running a repertoire of productions, eg English National Opera at The Coliseum, The Royal Opera House Covent Garden, The Royal National Theatre and also the Royal Shakespeare Theatre.

The RSC first experimented with an automated overhead lighting rig in their temporary Courtyard Theatre at Stratford–upon-Avon. Lighting galleries surrounded the three sides of the thrust stage with a limited number overhead leaving the grid space clear for flying of scenic pieces as well as actors. Therefore any additional luminaires to provide area and dramatic lighting effects had to be suspended within this space. Access was going to be a problem so the concept of clusters of moving heads suspended from the grid was the solution.

Clusters of two moving heads were mounted under a pallet that is stabilized by 'Lightlock', a system that was developed by the RSC to remove the pendulum effect created by the panning and tilting of the moving head on the suspended pallet. The concept of an automated lighting rig was developed and installed in the Royal Shakespeare Theatre. (See page 325 Automated lighting rigs)

Moving head cluster mounted on 'Lightlock' – Photo by Stewart Hemely © RSC

Electronic Motion Stabilizers

Electronic Motion Stabilizers EMS has been developed by some manufactures of Moving Heads to reduce the effect of movement of the head, absorbing vibrations from audio outputs, truss movement and sprung or suspended floors. EG Robe Bright Multi-functional Luminaire BMFL Spot.

Did you know that –

■ Pole operated lanterns were originally developed for use in Television studios and were the forerunner of moving lights

■ In 1981, the first automated lights were developed by a small North American company for the Genesis tour and they were named VARI*LITE by the band's manager; see www.Vari-lite/com 1981

■ In 1987, the Golden Scan was developed by a small Italian company Clay Paky. The company was named after its founder Pasquale Quadril who formerly played with his friend Claudio in a band that they nick-named 'Paky and Clay'. At that time there were few lighting effects so this young engineer decided to make his own using slide projectors and liquid oil wheels. This developed into a successful professional show lighting company producing a new generation of "intelligent" projectors. In 1999 'Stage Line' a moving body projector was launched;

6 DMX FIXTURES   A quick start

2004 the 'Alpha' Spot, Wash and Beam lights; 2010 'Sharpy' the first intense beam-light to be produced and 2013 B-EYE LED wash, beam effects light. The ownership of Clay Paky S.p.A. was transferred to OSRAM in August and Pasquale 'Paky' Quadri died in September 2014. This was a sad loss of an icon of the show lighting industry.

■ One of the first uses of moving heads in the UK was in the original production of the musical *Miss Saigon* at the Theatre Royal Drury Lane when lighting designer David Hersey found that there was very limited space left in the overhead stage rig for conventional lighting with all the flying pieces which included a working replica of a helicopter

■ Moving heads are sometimes called 'nodding buckets' and moving mirrors 'wiggles'

Moving heads makes & models – see Part 3: 'Lighting Resources – Technical info.'

More resources – go to

www.adblighting.com –	ADB Lighting Technologies
www.claypaky.it –	Clay Paky
www.etcconnect.com –	ETC
www.highend.com –	High End Systems
www.martin.com –	Martin
www.vari-lite.com –	Philips Vari-Lite
www.robelighting.com –	Robe Lighting
www.qmaxz.com –	Qmaxz Lighting

A quick start

6 DMX FIXTURES

More info – LED performance luminaires

LED luminaires are similar in many ways to generic lanterns or 'conventionals' although there are some interesting exceptions. Some fixtures have been developed as moving heads, others having automated zoom focusing. One manufacturer has developed a single LED light engine that can be transformed for any application by attaching an LED Cyc or Fresnel adaptor, a zoom or a fixed focus lens tubes. 'One light engine with unlimited possibilities'.

The following abbreviations are used for the different LEDs used in the luminaires:
RGB – red, green, blue; **A** – amber, **WW** – warm white, **NW** – neutral white, **TW** – tungsten white, **CW** – cool white, **TW** – tunable white or **VW** – variable white.

Five types of LED luminaires/fixtures

Wash light – static position

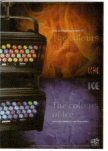

Fire & Ice – ETC

- **ETC Selador** – static: wash lights, 5 LED configurations: Lustre+, Palatta, Vivid-R, Fire & Ice each having their own unique dedicated colour range
- **Phillips Selecon PL3** – static: focusing wash light, variable beam angle, manual optical zoom – 3 x RGBW LED light engines
- **Robe Actor 3, 6 & 12 TM** – static wash lights – each having 19, 37 or 61 RGBW multichips independently controlled, motorized front lens zoom

Cyc light – static position

Source Four Cyc – ETC

- **Chauvet Ovation C-640FC** – RGBWA light engine
- **ETC Source Four CYC CE Adapter**: lens tube adapter for Source Four LED engine housing turning the beam through 45 degrees – 'x 7 Colour System'

6 DMX FIXTURES

More info

6 DMX FIXTURES · **More info**

Cyc light – static position

PLCYC2 Cyc Luminaire – Philips Selecon

- **Phillips Selecon PLCYC 1, PLCYC2** – RBGW LED light engine mounted through an asymmetrical reflector
- **Spotlight CYC LED 300**: true asymmetrical floodlight – RGBW LED light engines mounted within an asymmetrical reflector

Parlight – static position, parallel beam

Spectra Par 100 – Robert Altman

ColourSource PAR – ETC

- **Altman Spectra Par 100 & Spectra Star Par** – static: 4 interchangeable lenses, 4 configurations: RGBA, RGBW, 3K W, 3K – 6K TW LED engines
- **Chroma-Q: Color 100** – static: RGBA ColorSure
- **Coemar: Reflection FullSpectrum** – static: motorized zoom, modular multiple LEDs axial light source with parabolic reflector, built-in library of filter colours
  Refelection VariWhite – static: TW
- **ETC: ColourSource PAR** – static: 'x 7 Colour System' LED, 8 multichips
- **Martin Professional** – static: RUSH PAR 2 RGBW, RUSH PAR 2 WW/CW motorised zoom
- **J T S** – static: PixelPar quad RGBA, RGBW LEDS 10 degree
- **Selador Desire CE** – static: interchangeable beam angle lenses, round, linear, oblong fields, 5 configurations – **Lustre+, Palatta, Vivid-R, Fire & Ice**

Robin ParFect 100 – Robe

- **Robe: Robin ParFect 100** – static: 7 degree beam angle, 10, 20, 40 degrees diffusion filters, colour frame mounting & barndoor – RGBW LED, Tungsten emulation
- **Robe: Parfect S1** – static: 23 degree beam angle, colour frame mounting and barndoor – LED colour temperatures 6000k crisp white or 2700k warm white
- **Robe: Parfect H1** – static: 23 degree same specification as S1, controlled by conventional line voltage dimmer module

Fresnel – static position

Ovation F – Chauvet

PLFresnel 1 – Phillips Selecon

Source Four LED Fresnel Adapter – ETC

- **Chauvet Ovation F95** – static: adjustable Fresnel lens – WW LED engine
- **Coemar Reflection LEDko** – static: Soft Profile Fresnel manual zoom lens, 4 configurations – RGBW, WW, CW, VW LED engines
- **Philips Selecon PLFresnel 1** – static: adjustable Fresnel lens – RGBW LED engine
- **Philips Selecon RAMA LED** Fresnel – static: adjustable Fresnel lens, light output = 1/1.2K T.H. – 3000K LED engine, for use with colour filters
- **Robert Juliat ZEP-340F** 120mm, **TIBO-535** 200mm – static: adjustable fresnel lens, 4 configurations – WW, NW, CW & VW LED engines
- **ETC Source Four Fresnel Adapter** – static: lens tube adapter for Series 1 CE and Series 2 CC Lustr x7 Color & TW LED engines
- **Spotlight FresneLED** 100W, 200W, 600W – static: interchangeable Fresnel/PC lens, mains dim option, 3 configurations – WW, NW, CW LED engines
- **Spotlight FresneLED** 250W, 300W, 600W – static, TW or RGBW LED engines

6 DMX FIXTURES   More info

Fresnel/Variable Wash – moving head

VLX Wash – Philips Vari-Lite

Robin DLF Wash – Robe

- **Martin Professional Quantum Wash – moving head**: focusing zoom wash light, "Soft lens accessory makes the beam more compact and dense adding a 'Fresnel-ish' appearance – RGBW LED light engine

- **Phillips Vari-Lite**:

  VLX wash – moving head: 7 x RGBW LED chip sets independently controlled.

  VLX3 wash – moving head: focusing wash light, variable beam angle, motorized optical zoom – 3 RGBW LED chip set engines

- **Robe Robin DL4F Wash – moving head**: fresnel lens, motorized zoom with diffusion filter, internal barndoor four individually controllable blades with 90 degree rotation – RGBW, preselected whites and TW emulation

PC Prism Convex – static position

PCLED 200 – Spotlight

- **Coemar Reflection LEDko** – static: Soft Profile PC zoom lens – Four configurations: RGBW, WW, CW, VW LED engines

- **Spotlight PCLED** 100W, 200W, 600W – static: interchangeable PC/Fresnel lens, mains dim option, 3 configurations – WW, NW, CW LED engines.

- **Spotlight PCLED** 250W, 300W, 600W – static: RGBW or TW LED engines

6 DMX FIXTURES   **More info**

Profile spot – static position

LED Phoenix Profile Spot – Altman Lighting

Source Four LED series 2 – ETC

ProfiLED 150 RGBW – Spotlight

- **Altman LED Phoenix Profile spot** – static: 150W, 250W long throw, 4 configurations – RGBA, RGBW, WW, CW, LED light engines

- **Chauvet Ovation E-190** – static: zoom and fixed lens tubes – WW LED engine

- **Coemar Reflection LEDko** – static: Profile HD zoom lens, 4 configurations – RGBW, WW, CW, VW LED engines

- **ETC Source Four LED Series 1 CE** – static: zoom & a range of fixed lens tubes, 4 LED engines – Lustr+ x7 Color, Tungsten, Daylight, Studio HD

- **Source Four LED Series 2 CE** – static: zoom & a range of fixed lens tubes, 3 LED engines: Lustr array x7 Color, Tungsten HD, Daylight HD

- **Phillips Selecon**:

  PLProfile1 LED – static: zoom lens – RGBW LED light engine

  PLProfile4 LED – static: zoom and fixed lenses – RGBW LED light engine

- **Robert Juliat**:

  ZEP 640SX – static: zoom lens – 2 configurations – WW, CW LED engines

  TIBO 533 – static: condenser optical system, 3 configurations – WW, NW, CW LED engines

- **Spotlight**:

  ProfiLED 100 (mains dim option), **200** – static: zoom lens, 3 configurations – WW, NW, CW LED engines,

  ProfiLED 150/250 – static: zoom lens – RGBW LED engine

6 DMX FIXTURES

More info

Profile spot – moving head

MAC Quantum Profile – Martin Professional

DL4S Profile – Robe

■ **Martin Professional: MAC Quantum Profile – moving head**: motorized zoom, lens, effects wheels, CMY subtractive Colour Mixing System – W LED engine

■ **Robe: Robin DL4S Profile – moving head**: PC lens, motorized zoom, 4 variable speed individual framing shutters with 90 degree rotation, animation effects wheel, rotating gobos. – RGBW colour control with preselected whites and Tungsten lamp emulation

■ **Robe: DL7S Profile – moving head**: 800W, fast framing shutters, Selection of 6 rotating and 8 fixed gobos wheel selected for theatre use, 7 colour LED fully homogenised light module

Other LED fixtures

➤ **Linear LED Strips** consisting of a single line tricolour LEDs provides a linear colour mixing. The earlier versions suffered from producing a rainbow shadow effect that limited their use for the purposes of illumination. However they can be used for 'eye candy' effects as part of a set for musicals without dazzling the eyes.

Moving linear strips of LED modules with adjustable zoom and tilt mechanism can produce rapid sweeps of rainbow effect. The Robin 'CycFX' gives a whole new meaning to cyc batten but can fall short of providing a seamless wash. Martin Professional 'Tripix' uses *"tricolour LEDs for superior mixing at the lens – resulting in the absence of colour shading."*[34]

Linear strips can also be used to provide a colour wash for low level frontal fill light (footlights) or for a backing surface behind a window where there is limited space for a conventional lantern.

Tripix 300/12 – Martin Professional

Robin CycFX 8 – Robe

CycFX rainbow effects – Robe

[34] Martin Professional Website

More info

6 DMX FIXTURES

B-EYE K20 – Clay Paky   *Parallel beams and Kaleidoscopic projections – Clay Paky*

➤ **Moving head wash-lights** can produce some stunning colour and graphic effects. They consist of RGBW LED Multi-chips or Quads arranged in circular arrays radiating from a central multichip allowing endless colour variations and movements within the projected beam making it a virtual colour wheel. The beam angle can be zoomed in from a wide angled 'wash light' to a narrow 'beam fixture'. Fast moving mid-air parallel beam effects can be created with the moving head with projected micro–rays that can be individually controlled and coloured to produce a rotating and pulsating beam. On the Clay Paky 'A.LEDA B-EYE K20' the front lens can be rotated to produce lots of small dynamic bright compositions producing a kaleidoscopic projection. Robe produces a similar moving washlight the Robin 1000 LEDBeam. The John Thomas Engineering PixelSmart combines 12 quad RGBW 20 degree angle with 13 WW 11 degree angle LEDS capable of producing vast colour palette with a brilliant white core.

➤ **Light wall** units provide a low-energy alternative to conventional cyc lighting providing greater control over the total surface to paint a seamless colour mix by back lighting a screen or cloth. The space required for using Cyc lights above and below can be dramatically reduced from 2.000m to less than 500mm by using a light wall.

➤ **Martin EventLED wall** consists of one metre square panels, each containing 16 super wide-angled RGB Multicolor LEDs. The lightweight panels can be clipped together as a column or assembled as a wall behind a plastic back projection screen to diffuse the LED sources. The white surface of the EventLED panels acts as a bounce surface providing a very even distribution of the coloured light. A very wide range of colours can be produced from primary to pale tints, and graduated cyc colours, rainbows, sunsets, dissolves and wipes can be produced by having the ability to control the colour and intensity of each LED source.

EventLED – ABTT Sightline

Points for action

Quickies!
- View the products on the websites

Takes longer
- View Selador Fire & Ice demo video, go to www.etcconnect.com
- View LEE Filters Quick Videos 'Working with LED and Tungsten' go to – www.leefilters.com

A proper job!
- LED Lighting – for a brief history of LEDs and future developments, go to www.pixelrange.com
- Information on LED technology – www.wikipedia.org/wiki/Light-emitting_diode – Wikipedia

More info

6 DMX FIXTURES

Extras – LED technology

The development of the light-emitting diodes has provided a new low-energy light source for the design of theatre fixtures. LEDs have the advantage over traditional light sources in that they have a low energy consumption and longer lamp life. They have a considerable reduction in heat output as compared with theatre lanterns which is an important considerations for the 'green economy'.

LED sources of light

Light Emitting Diodes is a light source that uses the electroluminescence of a semiconductor to create light by the movement of electrons releasing photons that we see as light. The semiconductors are dyed using a laser technology to produce coloured LEDs. Initially red, green and yellow LEDs were only available and at first they were used as indicator lamps on electronic equipment. It took a long time before blue and finally white LEDs were able to be produced. Further developments have led to adding small reflectors to the semiconductor crystal and other components to make the light emitted brighter, focusing into a single point suitable for the use as a light source for illumination.[37]

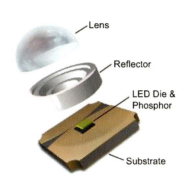

LED assembly – Thomas Nell Spotlight

➤ **RGB LEDs** – Red, Blue and Green LEDs emit three different, narrow peak frequencies of coloured light. They are rather like the spikes in a comb which creates a problem when trying to mix them to produce a range of colours. The three highly saturated primary colours will produce vibrant secondary colours when added and mixed together and in theory should produce white light. This method is called additive mixing – see page 148 'Primary colours of light'. However in practice when

RGB LEDs

mixed together it is difficult to create a true white light and pastel shades to match those produced when using colour filters with tungsten source lanterns.

➤ **LEDs – two forms of mixing RGB+W:**
- **Exterior mix** as used on LED strips and pixilated wash lights that are used mainly for producing vibrant 'eye candy' effects. However this method of mixing can produce a rainbow style shadow effect. It is difficult to produce a uniform beam

[37] Edison Tech Centre

of light and a good colour distribution with fixtures that use exterior mixing. Therefore they are not suitable for performance lighting, skin tones or producing white light but they can produce some dramatic moving pixilated effects.

■ **Interior mix** – TriColour TC, Multi-Colour MC are a single point source of either three RGB of four RCBW LED colour emitters combined in a single unit with a small fixed lens and an electro-optical system. They can be precisely controlled by a DMX signal to provide an accurate means of colour mixing and control, producing a clean source of light. A similar mixing system is used in LED engines that are used to provide the light source for the optical system used in LED luminaires.

Two different technologies

The manufacturers of LED fixtures have concentrated on developing LED light engines that can either produce a good mix of colour to replicate that produced by traditional colour filters with tungsten lamp sources or a pure monochromatic white light.

There are two different technologies being used:

➤ **Monochromaic white LEDs** produce a continuous full spectrum of white light that generates all the visible electromagnetic irradiations. This is produced by using LEDs with a high frequency blue dye with a phosphor coating that can convert the high energy blue light into one of the specific colour temperatures, 3000K – 4000K – 5600K to produce monochromatic white light. Each LED dye can only produce one fixed frequency of electromagnetic irradiation and therefore is unable to make a colour shift which occurs when dimming tungsten halogen lamps.

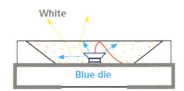

LED cross-section showing blue dye and white phosphor coating – Thomas Nell Spotlight

Chip on Board – Spotlight

The monochromatic white light is created by a 'Chip on Board' COB having a number of blue dyed LEDs each having a different phosphor coating to provide a mix of monochromatic white light. The LEDs are individually controlled by an LED driver and can be tuned to achieve a colour temperature shift from 3000K to 5600K. This produces a continuous monochromatic white spectrum that is free from the rainbow shadow effects that can be detected by television cameras. This makes them suitable for illuminating the face and for use in TV Studio. They can also be tuned to simulate the colour shift when being dimmed to emulate a Tungsten light source of 3200K matching the output of tungsten lanterns and therefore can be used with the standard range of colour filters. Some manufacturers call these LEDs Variable White VW but Tunable White TW is a more specific term.[38]

[38] *Source* – Thomas Nell, Spotlight

Colour temperatures: Tunable white light measured in Kelvins

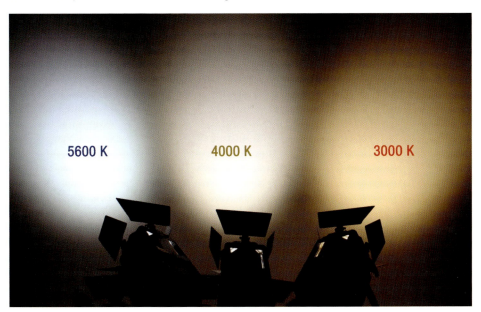

Monochromatic Whites – Thomas Nell Spotlight

CW Cool White	**NW** Neutral White	**Tungsten**	**WW** Warm White
5600K	4000K	3200K	3000K

➤ RGB+W, RGB +A LEDs:

- RGB+W use the same COB chip design. The white LED adds the missing electromagnetic frequencies of visible colours smoothing out the peaks in the RGB mix. The emitters can be tune to produce softer pastel shades that are good for skin tones and reproduce a wide range of colours as found in filter swatch books.
- RGB+A adds Amber to the RGB mix producing more vibrant colours
- RGB+W, RGB+A can be tuned to create white light but it does not produce a true monochromatic full spectrum white free from rainbow shadows that can be detected by TV cameras. Therefore it is not suitable for use in TV studios.

Variations in the development of RGB technology

➤ 7 Colour chip sets:

ETCs Selador 'x7 Colour' chip set LED System uses 7 coloured LED emitters adding Indigo, Cyan, Lime and Amber to Red, Green and Blue to smooth out the spikes of colour produced when mixing RGB to give colour mixing to match the conventional range of colour filters. The addition of a lime-green emitter increases the lumen output in open white and lighter colour tints.[39]

[39] *Source Four LED 'Lighting that's believable' – ETC*

6 DMX FIXTURES   Extras!

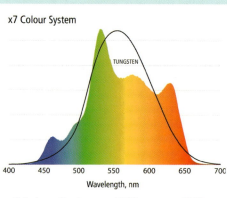
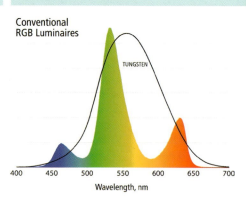

x 7 Colour System vs RGB array – ETC

➤ **Reflection LEDko technology**

Coemar's Reflection technology produces a homogeneous light beam by mixing the light at the source through a newly developed micro-optical system. By mixing light at source Reflection LEDko replaces the multi-lens diode based technology.

The Reflection *'FullSpectrum' luminaire projects the 'Multi-LED' light source into a rear-facing parabolic reflector to produce a uniform beam with no pixels or dots.*

➤ **Prism mixing**

Robe use a prism for mixing the RGBW sources into a single focused beam of light and have developed a 7 colour LED engine for their DL7S profile spot providing *imperceptable high definition colour mixing.*[40]

The development of LED luminaires

The early luminaires were retrofits with LED engines inserted into existing profile spot lantern housing using the tungsten halogen optical system which was not entirely successful.

There were six major problems to solve in the research and development of LED Light Engines and luminaires:

■ Developing electronic dimming to provide a smooth curve down to zero without any flicker and shift in the colour temperature and sudden drop out at the end

■ Developing multiple arrays of LEDs to provide a seamless range of colours to match the colours produced by the range of colour filters used with tungsten halogen lamps in conventional generic lanterns. To achieve this manufacturers have used different arrays of LEDs;
RGB+W commonly being used in luminaires by a number manufacturers,
RGB+A (Amber) – Robert Altman,
'**x7 Color chip set LED System**' – ETC.

[40] Robe News Prolight & Sound 2015

Extras!

6 DMX FIXTURES

Others have produced luminaires with **CW, NW, WW & TW** LED engines to provide a range of white light colour temperatures and to emulate tungsten sources that can be used with LED filters – Coemar, Martin, Robert Juliat & Spotlight.

- The design of optical systems to accommodate LED light engines

- The design of lantern housings to accommodate the LED engines and to accept existing front lens tubes – Coemar, ETC & Selecon

- Developed new optical systems – Spotlight & Martin Professional and new concepts with automated focus and shutter systems mounted in a moving heads – Vari-Lite & Robe

- To produce a quiet fan assisted cooling system[41]

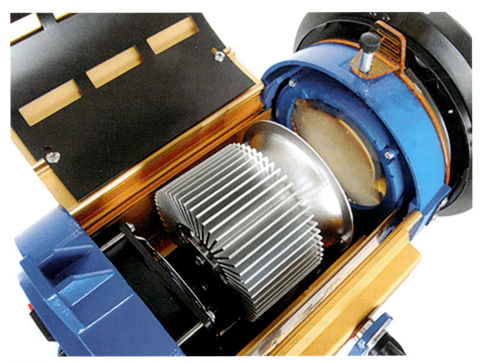

LED Engine in optical housing – Spotlight

[41] Thomas Nell – Spotlight

6 DMX FIXTURES   Extras!

7 Health & Safety

A quick start – Good working practice

Safety checks when working with lanterns, using access systems and working at heights

More info – Access equipment

Using access systems, portable step ladders and platform equipment

Extras! – H&S policies & risk assessment

Understanding and carrying out a risk assessment

A quick start – Good working practice

There are many potential hazards when working with lighting equipment. It is important to use safe working practices and to be aware of the dangers when working on the stage or in the studio.

> ❯ **Online video link – 7.1: Safety when working at heights**
> https://vimeo.com/123717496

Safety checklists

The following checklist is provided as a guideline for safe working practices and user awareness. It is not a replacement for the current legislation and relevant health and safety recommendations which are the responsibility of the manager of the theatre space to enforce.

➤ **Electrical safety** – check that:
  ☑ **Portable Appliance Tests** have been carried out on all the lanterns and cables in the last 12 months.[42] Check the date on the green test stickers usually attached to the plug top or on the equipment
  ☑ Regular visual 'user checks' have been made on all the lanterns and cables. Look for the common faults; damage to outer cable insulation and exposure of internal cables at the point of entry to lanterns, plug tops and cable sockets

[42] IEE Electrical Maintenance including Portable Appliance Testing

7 HEALTH AND SAFETY   A quick start

✓ **Periodic Electrical Test** of the installation including the lighting bars has been made during the last year (Places of Entertainment) and within the last five years (Educational Establishments)[43]

If the equipment and installation hasn't been checked or is faulty, don't use it; refer it to your technical manager or chief electrician.

➤ **Safety when working with lanterns** – check that:

✓ The hanging clamp is correctly fitted to the lantern and that the top bolt is tight

✓ A safety bond is permanently attached to the anchor point or hanging bracket of each lantern to prevent it falling off when being unclipped from the lighting bar

✓ The safety clip is used to prevent the colour frames and barndoors from falling out of the colour runners

✓ The shortest length of cable is used without creating any obvious hazards, as a long cable has the risk of compromising the earth impedance which could be fatal

✓ Extension cables are not coiled as they can overheat

➤ **Safety when working at heights**

✓ Wear strong, non-slip rubber-soled shoes and have no loose clothing to catch on obstructions

✓ A Bump Hat should be worn for protection when working under hanging equipment

✓ A hard hat should be worn when working in the area below an access system

✓ Tools should not be carried in a pocket but carried on belt clip, held in a 'tool belt' or attached to a lanyard around the neck

✓ If you drop anything, shout 'Heads', as this is a recognised signal

✓ Equipment should be rigged on flown bars at stage level and then raised into position

✓ On fixed bars lanterns can be raised and lowered by using a strong rope over the bar

✓ Use a karabiner to clip on to the lantern; always use a bowline knot to attach it to the hauling line[44]

✓ Wear a hard hat and use protective gloves when raising and lowering equipment on a rope

✓ Never carry lanterns single-handed up a ladder

Bump Hat – GMSL

Hard hat – GMSL

[43] IEE Electrical Maintenance including Portable Appliance Testing
[44] Karabiner & bowline, see 'Lighting jargon – Rigging'

➤ **Using access systems**

The following points should be checked by a trained supervisor but as an operator it is always worth checking these points for your own personal safety:

- ☑ **It is suitable for the intended work** providing a safe working height to reach the lanterns and supports the upper body without overreaching
- ☑ **It is correctly erected** and 'signed off' by a certified trained operator
- ☑ **It is correctly positioned** to prevent overreaching sideways so that the operator's 'belt buckle' stays within the width of the ladder or access system when working
- ☑ **The work area** below is clear of obstructions and additional people who might cause distractions

➤ **As the operator** – when using the access system:

- ☑ **A supervisor should be present** who has received relevant training on the equipment
- ☑ **You should have received adequate training** over the safe use of the access equipment before being allowed to use it
- ☑ **Never work alone** – always have somebody working with you to assist in raising and lowering equipment and to summon help if there is an accident

Above all, use your head when working at heights and be safe

QUICK TIPS

- ■ Electrical safety and testing is the responsibility of the manager of the facilities
- ■ **If you haven't been trained, don't use the access equipment**
- ■ Wear a Bump Hat when rigging, angling and focusing to protect your head
- ■ Never leave tools on the platform of an access system as they could fall when it is moved
- ■ Wear a hard hat when working below a ladder, tower or access system
- ■ If you hear 'Heads!', don't look up but just get out of the way

Points for action

Quickies!

- ■ Check out the Health & Safety policy for your performance space

More info – Access equipment

It is important to understand the safety requirements and to establish good working practice when using access systems.

The following information is provided purely as a guideline for safe working practices and user awareness. It is not a replacement for the current legislation and relevant health and safety recommendations which are the responsibility of the technical manager of the theatre space to enforce.

Portable ladders – Step, extension & combination ladders

Designed to be used to provide access for light maintenance work and not as a working platform.

The following points need to be considered before using a ladder:
- The type of the work that is to be carried out on the ladder
- In the UK the Work at Height Regulations 2004 (WAHR) states that:
  'ladders can be used as workplaces when it is not reasonably practicable to use other potentially safer means and the Risk Assessment shows that risks are low'
- Check that the ladder meets the European standards: BS EN 131 for Light Trade use, a BS 2037 Class 3 Domestic ladder sold in shops for DIY work should **not be used**
- The ladder must be the right height for the job to prevent overreaching, and to provide support for the upper body, observe the belt buckle limits; see 'A quick start'
- **Three points of body contact should be maintained at all times:** that is, both feet and one hand, which limits the safe working use of a ladder mainly to adjusting lanterns but not rigging

Three types of portable step ladders

➤ **Step ladders** provide a stable free-standing A-frame. When using a step ladder, the upper body should be supported at all times by the ladder or hand rail; therefore, it is important not to stand on the two steps immediately below the top. The step ladder should be positioned at 90 degrees to the work and never used sideways-on as it will be unstable.

➤ **Extension ladders** should be used on a firm level floor with the top resting on a stable, strong surface and not against a lighting bar. It should be inclined at the safe vertical base angle of 75 degrees using the one-to-four rule, 1 unit out at the base for 4 units high, and secured to prevent slippage by anchoring at the top or 'footing' at the bottom by another person.

Step ladder – GMSL

➤ **Combination ladders** – Zarges Skymaster is a three-part extension ladder, which can be assembled to provide a free-standing braced A-frame with an overhanging extended section providing additional access. However, the safest position is to stand either on the apex of the 'A' frame or one rung up with the upper body supported by the extended ladder. Therefore, it is worth considering the average working height when purchasing a Zarges ladder. Footing the A-frame will provide extra stability and reassurance for the user.

Zarges Skymaster

Platform equipment – Towers & ESCA

A working platform system provides safe access for angling and focusing and rigging of lanterns on lighting bars.

➤ **Towers**
- **Stabilisers/outriggers must be used at all times** to provide adequate stability and the brakes set before the equipment is used
- The stabilisers and brakes need to be released before they can be moved; therefore, the equipment should not be moved with an operator on the working platform. This means the operator must climb up and down every time the equipment is to be moved
- Equipment to be rigged should only be lifted within the footprint of the equipment and not be hauled up outside

➤ **Mobile towers** – Single-width 1.2m or 1.5m wide rectangular ladder frame aluminium tower can be easily positioned alongside lighting bars and take up less space than the double-width square platforms. All towers should be fitted with internal ladders, a full-width platform deck having a trap door access, kickboards and safety rails. Stabilisers/outriggers should be used on towers where the working platform is over 2m, i.e. one unit high. It should never be moved while there is an operator on the platform over 2m high.

Mobile tower – Instant UpRight UK

➤ **An ESCA mobile access platform** has a wide, stable wheeled base that doesn't require the use of outriggers. It can be driven and manoeuvred by the operator from the work platform, saving time and the need to climb up and down as with other systems, and is a safe system to use only on a flat stage. The ESCA is compact and is easily stored ready for use.

ESCA – ESCA UK

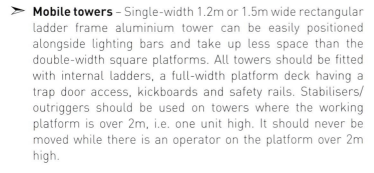

Tallescope

➤ A Tallescope is a telescopic aluminium manually operated work platform which is supported on a wheeled base and accessed by a vertical ladder. It should only be used with stabilisers/outriggers in place and not moved with the operator on the work platform. Tallescopes are not particularly suitable for rigging lanterns as distinct from focusing as lanterns cannot be safely lifted within the footprint of the equipment.[45]

➤ **'The Code of Practice for the use of Tallescopes for working at heights in theatres' (2014) states:**

Tallescope – Aluminium Access Products Ltd

- *"**5.72**: Deploy the outriggers, two along each side as near as possible to 60 degrees to the long axis of the Tallescope to gain maximum stability. .... except when working on rakes, it is reasonable with light work such as focusing .... To set the outrigger's feet 10mm above the surface."*
- *"**5.91**: ....Moving a Tallescope with a technician in the cage is only justifiable where the risk assessment deems it less hazardous to remain in the cage than risk fatigue and associated likelihood of slipping or falling from the access ladder or when climbing in and out of the cage and the additional precautions are in place."*[46]

➤ **The Three Fours:**

A. ***Four push-pull post*** *so operators do not have to bend at the waist and can steer more easily and with a better view*

B. ***Four non-lift castors fitted*** *so not to cause any movements in the Tallescope when the brakes are being engaged or disengaged. The brakes should be applied when the Tallescope is not in motion*

C. ***Four outriggers*** *reduce the possibility of the Tallescope falling sideways. The outriggers are locked off with the feet not more than 10mm above the floor.*[47]

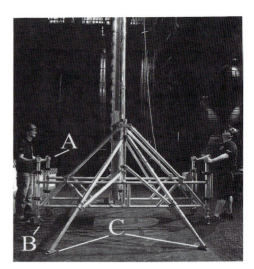

Tallescope showing three fours – ABTT Sightline

[45] David Adams Chairman ABTT Safety Committee
[46] ABTT Code of practice for the selection and use of temporary access equipment for working at height in theatres
[47] ABTT revised Code of Practice on Work at height in theatres – Sightline Autumn 2011

➢ **Movement of a Tallescope** with an operator in the cage is therefore very restricted and should only be carried out under direct supervision. The code of practice requires a full risk assessment to be carried out (see Health & Safety – Extras).

"There are many hazards on stage when scenery is in place that makes the safe movement of a Tallescope with a technician in the basket impractical with the outriggers in place. 10mm is the specified maximum clearance of the outriggers feet above the surface. It has been found that if this is increased to 100mm then the forces applied at the cage level due to the weight of the technician are shifted outside of the wheelbase and that it is likely to significantly decrease the stability of the Tallescope even when the ladder is not fully extended."[48]

➢ **Tallescope rescue kits** have been developed in order to safely lower an injured technician in the basket to ground level.

MORE TIPS

■ Always use stabilisers/outriggers on mobile towers with a working platform over one unit or 2m high
■ Never climb up on the outside of a tower as this can make it unstable
■ Never move a mobile tower with an operator on the work platform

---

Technical info. – in the UK

'Code of Practice – working at heights in theatres' (2011) ABTT – Association of British Theatre Technicians
'Code of practice for use of Tallescopes for working at heights in theatres' (2014) ABTT – Association of British Technicians
'Health and Safety Regulation … a short guide': HSE – Health and Safety Executive
'Safe Use of Ladders & Stepladders: an employers' guide': HSE
HSE information sheet on tower scaffolds: HSE
'Use Your Head for Heights stay within the Law': The Ladder Association – http://ladderassociation.org.uk
'Operators' Code of Practice for prefabricated towers': PASMA – Prefabricated Access Suppliers' & Manufacturers' Association
Tallescope Rescue Kit video clip – Aluminium Access Products

7 HEALTH AND SAFETY

More info

---

[48] 'Tall(escope) tales' Paul Edwards – ABTT Sightline Autumn 2011

➤ **Risk assessment when working at heights**
This should cover:

- **Possible dangers** and the level of risk involved
- **Suitability of the equipment** available to carry out the job
- **Risk of incorrect assembly** of the access system
- **Positioning and use** of the equipment for all aspects of the space
- **List of who is trained** to use the access systems

Conducting a risk assessment – there are four stages:

1. **Identifying the hazard/risk – Before assessment**
   - List the hazards/risks
   - Assess each hazard/risk identified, the probability of an accident occurring and the severity of an injury on a 1 low–5 high scale
   - Calculate the risk factor – probability x severity

2. **Recommending precautions**
   - Assess the risk factors – low, medium, high
   - Identify items to be improved, where further action is required and immediate action needs to be taken
   - Recommend and list the precautions to be taken

3. **Reviewing the hazard/risk – After assessment**
   - Assess the recommended precautions
   - Assess the probability of an accident occurring and severity of an injury based on the recommended precautions to be taken on a 1–5 scale
   - Calculate the risk factor – probability x severity
   - Identify any further improvements, further action or immediate action to be taken
   - List further action required

4. **Feedback and communication**
   - Review the 'Further action to be taken'
   - Ensure that those supervising and undertaking the work know and act on the recommended precautions

HEALTH & SAFETY – *Risk Assessment*	Venue: Sundial Theatre Cirencester College [50]						
Activity	**Fit-up** – *Alice in Wonderland*						
Description of operation	**Stage** – Using mobile tower to rig lanterns over stage 5m height						
Who is affected by this operation?	Staff	X	Students	X	Public		Others

Description of hazards/risk – Before	Probability Accident 1–5	Severity injury 1–5	Risk Factor P x S
Assembly	3	5	15
Stabilisers	3	5	15
Hazards on-stage	4	2	8
Edge of raised stage	3	5	15
Climbing access equipment	3	4	12
Danger of low-hanging equipment	3	2	6
Raising lanterns/luminaires	4	3	12
Carrying tools	4	3	12
Working below access system	4	3	12
Moving access system	5	5	25

Probability	1 Very unlikely	2 Unlikely	3 Could occur	4 Likely	5 Will occur
Severity/injury	1 Very minor	2 Minor	3 Serious	4 Major	5 Fatal
Risk Factors	Multiply Probability x Severity to obtain Risk Factor				

Risk factor **Low 0–6**	Risk factor **Medium 7–14**	Risk factor **High 15–25**
Above 5 – improve if possible	Above 10 – further action required	15 + immediate action required

Recommended precautions

1 Tower to be assembled and signed off by certified operator
2 Outriggers to be in position and used at all times while operator is on the platform
3 Stage to be cleared of any minor or major obstructions
4 Edge of stage to be marked with hazard tape
5 Internal ladders to be used to access platform

[50] Based on an H&S model from Central School of Speech and Drama

7 HEALTH AND SAFETY

Extras!

6 Bump Hat or hard hat to be worn by operator
7 Lanterns/luminaires to be passed hand to hand to the operator by technicians using the internal ladders
8 Tools to be clipped to operator's belt
9 Area below access system to be kept clear and hard hats to be worn
10 Tower to be moved by min two operators and third to direct passage

Description of hazards/risk – After	Probability Accident 1–5	Severity Injury 1–5	Risk After 1–5
1 Assembly	1	1	1
2 Stability	1	1	1
3 Hazards on stage	1	1	1
4 Edge of raised stage	1	1	1
5 Climbing access equipment	2	5	10 *
6 Danger of low-hanging equipment	3	1	2
7 Raising lanterns/luminaires	2	3	6 *
8 Carrying tools	2	3	6 *
9 Working below access system	2	2	4
10 Moving access system	2	3	6 *

Further action to be taken *

5 Climbing access equipment – ensure that the students are supervised by qualified staff at all times

7 Raising lanterns/luminaires – ensure that the students are supervised by qualified staff at all times

8 Carrying tools – ensure that students are supervised by qualified staff at all times

10 Moving access system – ensure that students are supervised by qualified staff at all times

Lighting jargon – What's it called?

The language of stage lighting is a combination of electrical terms, practical descriptive words and historical theatre terms that have been drawn together over the years. It is important to become familiar with the terms as they are the common form of communication in the theatre industry.

➤ Lanterns – performance luminaires

Adjustable Focus	Lanterns that can be focused and the beam size adjusted
Axial Ellipsoidal	Adjustable focus lantern, semi-hard/soft edged precise beam, lamp mounted along the central axis of the lantern
Cyc – asymmetrical	Fixed beam flood, soft edged even wash directed downwards by an asymmetrical reflector
Ellipsoidal lantern	Adjustable focused lantern having an elliptical reflector
Fixed beam	Lanterns having a reflector and a lamp but no lens system
Fixed Focus	A profile lantern having one lens and a fixed beam angle
Flashing through	Checking that all the lanterns in the rig are working
Flood – symmetrical	Fixed focus lantern, soft edged even wash having a symmetrical reflector
Fresnel	Adjustable focus lantern, soft edged diffused beam with more spill light than a PC
Generic lanterns	Non-automated lanterns often referred to as Generics
Grid	The area above the stage from which lighting bars and scenery are suspended or flown
Instrument	Performance lighting unit, a term commonly used in North America
Lantern	Performance lighting unit, a traditional term used in the UK; see Luminaire, Instrument or Fitting
LEKO (NA)	Common name given to Ellipsoidal lanterns in North America
Luminaire	International general term used by lighting engineers for lighting equipment
Movers	Moving lights, automated fixtures
Multicore cable	A flexible cable having a number of singly insulated cores that can carry a number of mains lighting circuits or sound signals
Parcan	Fixed focus lantern, intense near parallel oval beam of light which can be rotated
Patching	The process of temporarily linking one circuit to another
PC/Plano-convex	Adjustable focus lantern, sharp edged beam of light, no spill light, used in Europe
PC/Prism/Pebble	Adjustable focus lantern, hard/semi-soft edged intense beam with less spill light than a Fresnel
Profile spotlight	Adjustable focus lantern, semi-hard/soft edged precise beam
Socaplex	A 19 core multicore mains extension cable providing six lighting circuits

129

Dimmer	Controls the amount of electricity going to a lamp and the intensity of the light
Dimmer pack	6 dimmer units usually having 6 pairs of outlet sockets mounted in a portable pack – '**6/12 channels**' (NA)
Dimmer rack	Dimmer units mounted in a rack; the outlet circuits are usually hardwired
Hard patch	Connecting the circuits from the lanterns to a dimmer unit via a hardwired socket distribution box or direct to a socket mounted on the dimmer
Voltage 'V'	Measurement of the electrical pressure or force of the mains supply
Watts 'W'	Measurement of the amount of electrical power, e.g. the power of the lamp in a lantern
Wattage	Power consumption of a lamp providing a rough guide to the intensity of light produced
Ohms	Measurement of resistance in an electrical conductor

➤ Lighting control desks

Analogue	Low-voltage control system connecting the control desk to the dimmers
Black Out – BO	Switch everything off
Chase	Continuous repeated sequence of flashing lights produced by the effects function on a lighting control desk as used on neon signs
Channel fader	Part of a control desk that operates an individual dimmer channel
Control desk	Alternative name Lighting Console
Dipless crossfade	Channel levels, set at the same level on both presets, remain at the same intensity and are not affected by the crossfade
DMX 512	Digital Multiplex – a high-speed data control system connecting the control desk, dimmers and fixtures
Flashing through	Raising each control channel in succession to check that the lantern or fixture is working after rigging and before each performance – '**Stepping through**' (NA)
Master Fader	Having the overriding control of a group of channel faders
Scene Preset	Group of individual faders on a lighting control desk that control the dimmers
Soft patch	Assigning a control channel on the lighting desk to the DMX address of a dimmer unit or piece of equipment

➤ Other abbreviations & terms

CIE	Commission Internationale de L'Eclairage produced the international lantern symbols
CMY	Cyan/Magenta/Yellow secondary colour filters used for colour mixing on moving heads together for subtractive mixing to produce additional colours

What's it called?

LIGHTING JARGON

Cyclorama/Cyc	White rear wall or backcloth used to mix coloured light & create sky effects
FOH	Front of house, the area used by the audience in front of the curtain or stage
LED	Light emitting diode
NICEIC	UK's electrical contracting industry's independent voluntary body for electrical installation contractors
Receiving House	A theatre in the UK that receives tours and doesn't mount their own productions, formerly known as a 'touring theatre' graded No1, No2 etc depending upon the size of the show that they received.
RGBW	Red, Green, Blue, White LED emitters used for colour mixing

LIGHTING JARGON

What's it called?

Colour, Gobos & Effects

Some useful additions – *looking at using colour, gobos, projecting slides and moving images, creating special effects, flashes and bangs!*

8 Colour filters

A quick start – Working with colour filters

Establishing good working practice when cutting and storing colour filters

More info – Filters, diffusion & reflection materials

Looking at the range of colour, technical filters and materials used in the theatre, film and television industries

Extras! – Coloured light

How filters work, colour temperature, correction filters and the effects of mixing coloured light

A quick start – Working with colour filters

Colour is created from white light by filtering out all the other colours from the spectrum. A colour filter inserted in a lantern doesn't colour the light; it filters out and absorbs all the other colours from the white light, allowing the single colour to project through.

Identifying colour filters

Colour filters are identified by a reference number and name, e.g. 002 – Rose Pink. Lighting designers and technicians refer to them by their number for ease of use.

➤ **Colour swatches**
Samples of colour filters can be obtained from the manufacturers in the form of a colour swatch. Some manufacturers, LEE and Rosco, include correction filters, diffusion and

*e-colour+
– Roscolab*

reflective materials that are used for film, video and TV with the colour effect filters in their swatch books.

➤ **Two types of colour swatches:**
The filters are organised in two ways:

■ **Numeric edition:** arranged in the order that each filter has been produced and not in a colour order. Very useful for identifying colours by the reference number when working from a lantern plan

■ **Chromatic/Designer editions:** arranged in their colour order grouped together in bands of colour making it easier to select colours

Cutting and storing filters

It is important to establish an organised method of cutting and storing colour filters as there are a large number of colours and many different sizes required to match all the lantern colour frames. Colour filters need to be accurately cut to fit the size of colour frame. Too small and the filter will buckle and distort under the heat; too large and it won't fit the frame.

➤ **Colour filter sheet sizes:**
■ Small sheets – 53cm x 61cm
■ Large sheets – 53cm x 122cm
■ Rolls – 122cm x 762cm

➤ **Identifying filters:**
■ The sheets of colour filters are usually marked with the colour number on a sticker on the right-hand edge of the sheet. Also the number is often printed on the tissue backing paper
■ Sheets of colour filters are difficult to identify so always make sure that they are clearly numbered
■ Mark the colour name and colour number on the sheet with a chinagraph or grease pencil

➤ **Cutting filters:**
■ It is important to know the exact dimension of the frame that fits the appropriate lantern
■ Always cut from the opposite edge to the number marked on the sheet
■ Mark the colour number in the top right corner of the cut filter for ease of identification
■ Do not mark the number in the middle as this can affect the life of the filter

➤ **Three methods of cutting:**
- Templates will help to cut the filter to the correct size; allow 5mm clearance in each direction to fit the colour into the frame
- Finger sheet cutters are a quick way to cut the pieces
- Use a paper trimmer when cutting a large number of pieces
- Never cut filters using an open-bladed knife and a steel rule, as the knife can easily slip off the steel rule and cut the supporting fingers or hand. This is a potential safety hazard

Sheet cutter – LEE Filters

➤ **Storing filters:**
- Store in single folders clearly marked with the colour number and name
- **It is easier to find colours if they are grouped together**

Neutrals –	Lavenders, Lilac, Pale Violet tints, Chocolate
Tints and Pastels –	Light Blues, Greens, Golds, Pinks & Roses, Ambers
Saturated Colours –	Deep Blues, Reds, Greens

- Use either a filing cabinet or a large-sized (A4) ring folder with clear plastic envelopes and white backing sheets for smaller-sized colours

➤ **Cutting filters with a paper trimmer:**
Paper trimmers provide a safe and accurate method of cutting filters. They are good for cutting single pieces but it is difficult to measure and cut multiple pieces continuously off a strip using the measuring rule mounted on the trimmer.

A simple extension board can be added on to the right-hand side of the trimmer to provide a way of measuring on the opposite side:

- Cut a board to fit on the side of the trimmer
- Measure from the cutting edge and mark the distance for each colour frame on the extension board with a suitable marker pen. Draw the sizes of the colour frame on the extension board
- Feed the strip under the pressure bar from the left, measured to size, marked on the right-hand side. Hold down the pressure bar and cut. Continue to cut to feed the strip from the left-hand side, measure and cut

Paper trimmer – GMSL

Did you know that -

- Colour filters were originally made from dyed gelatine, hence some still call modern filters 'gels'
- Rosco began producing gelatine filters in 1910 and cinemoid filters in the 1950s[2]
- Cinemoid, a self-extinguishing cellulose acetate material, replaced gelatine
- Colour filters are now made from surface-coated or deep-dyed polyester
- The Cinemoid range of colours Nos.1–59 were produced in the 1950s and were arranged in fairly good colour progression/order
- This original range was renumbered 101–159 and new colours have been added as they have been developed, before and after the first 60 colours, making the colour order far more random
- LEE Filters was founded in the late 1960s to meet the demands of the film industry, pioneering the use of modern polymeric materials to produce filters for film, TV and theatre
- 'A common old theatre joke was to get the "new boy" to wash the dusty "Gels" which would dissolve in the water and leave a colourful mess!'[3] Possibly more of an American practice?

MORE TIPS

- Polyester-coated filters have an approximate life of between 6 and 10 hours
- Never mix different makes or types of colour filters on scroll as they shrink at different rates
- When using dichroic filters, it is important to follow the manufacturer's instructions
- 'No one makes a Chocolate colour filter like GAM!'[4]
- Try LEE 742 Bram Brown, 'Dirtier than 156 Chocolate, good for skin tones. Dims well and doesn't go pink at low light levels.' Designed by Paule Constable[5]

---

[2] 'Guide to Colour Filters' Rosco
[3] Ziggy Jacobs – American Lighting Design student
[4] Ziggy Jacobs – American Lighting Design student
[5] LEE 700 Designer Series

More resources – go to

www.leefilters.com – Click on 'Resources' – 'Lighting Resources' – scroll down to 'Think LEE' & 'Poster Book' for 'Lighting Filter Comparator' chart

www.rosco.com – 'Colour the Industry Standard' – Roscolab poster comparing the Rosco Supergel, Rosco E- Colour+ and LEE Filters range of colours

www. rosco.com – 'The First Name in Colour' – Roscolab poster comparing the Rosco E-Colour+ and Supergel, also Roscolux, Supergel and E-Colour range of colours

GLOBAL JARGON

■ **Colour filter** (UK) – **'Gel'** is a commercial term used in North America

Points for action

Quickies!

■ Log on to www.leefilters.com: Click on Resources/Lighting Resources, scroll down to 'LEE Filters Quick Start Videos'. View: 'LEE Swatch App', 'Working with LED & Tungsten', 'Colour Correction Filters'

■ Try using the colour number reference system in the LEE Filters Designer edition

■ Look at the range of dichroic glass filters on the manufacturers' websites

8 COLOUR FILTERS   **More info**

➤ **Primary colours of light:** Red, Blue and Green
- For primary colours, use LEE/Rosco E-Colour+: 106 – Red, 120 – Deep Blue, 139 – Primary Green
- When the three primary coloured beams overlap, they all combine to produce white light
- Where two of the primary colours overlap, they combine to produce a secondary colour
- A whole series of colours can be created by varying the intensity of light of the three colours

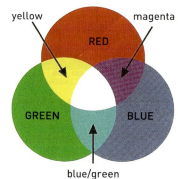

Primary colours – Strand Electric

➤ **Secondary colours:** Yellow, Magenta and Cyan (Blue/Green)

- Yellow produced by combining red and green light
- Magenta produced by combining red and blue light
- Blue/Green by combining green and blue light
- Secondary filter numbers LEE/Rosco E-Colour+: 101 – Yellow, 116 – Medium Blue/Green, 113 – Magenta
- These are also known as complementary colours

➤ **Complementary colours**
The colour triangle shows the three primary colours and the secondary colours that are created by mixing two of the primary colours.

White light is created by mixing a primary colour with the opposite secondary coloured light on the triangle in equal quantities:

- Red + Blue/Green = white light
- Green + Magenta = white light
- Blue + Yellow = white light

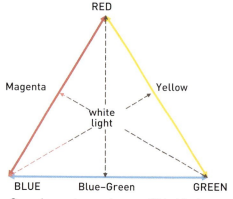

Complementary colours – Skip Mort

This effect works in reverse when a coloured light is projected on to a coloured pigment (paint or coloured material) **turning it black**

- Primary Red filtered light on to a Blue/Green material or painted surface will turn it black
- Blue/Green filtered light on to a primary red pigment will turn it black

Therefore, consideration needs to be given when selecting colours as to the effect that they may have on skin tones, the colours of the costumes, set and the stage surface.

Designers on colour – *'The practicalities of my approach are based simply upon realisation that if I take the spectrum apart with filters, then I can put that spectrum together again by superimposing the filter light beams. It is a gloriously unscientific process; not so much a rule-of-thumb as one of crossed fingers. And trusting my eyes.'* Francis Reid[8]

Did you know that -

- The colour reflection effect of red light turning green surfaces black and red light turning green black was first used by Adrian Samoiloff in 1922 at the London Hippodrome to create transformation scenes being used with costumes and backcloths. It was called the 'Samoiloff Effect' after him[9]
- Strips of colour dipped bulbs/lamps in primary colours were originally used to provide coloured lighting over the stage. They were wired in three or four circuits to give red, green, blue and white light
- The strips were replaced with the development of the three- and four-way compartment batten with clear lamps mounted with a reflector in individual compartments having a slot in front for a colour frame. Coloured lamps were replaced by 'Gels' – gelatine filters
- Compartment battens were used over the stage and as footlights with secondary colours to provide colour washes and to mix white light. A fourth 'open white' circuit was often used to provide additional illumination
- 'Full up to finish'[10] was a common term used in a lighting plot for musicals. On a major musical number, the main singers would be picked with the Limes (follow spots) and the stage lighting would be faded to a colour wash to provide the mood. On the climax at the end of the number, all the stage lighting would be raised to full, followed by the audience's applause
- With the introduction of the use of spotlights and Floods over the stage, the compartment battens were reduced to being used to light skycloths and backcloths
- The cyc colours were originally mixed from primary or secondary colours in a three-way compartment batten. Four-way battens were used to provide an extra set of blue filters to increase the intensity
- As the range of colour filters increased, lighting designers started to select individual colours to mix and produce the desired colour on the cyc or skycloth
- Colour cyc lighting on major shows is now produced using LED light walls

[8] Rosco Guide to Colour Filters – Designers on Colour
[9] *The Art of Stage Lighting*, Frederick Bentham
[10] David Edmund, Stage Manager, Theatre Royal Exeter

8 COLOUR FILTERS   Extras!

GLOBAL JARGON

■ **Compartment battens** (UK) – **'Cyc lights'**, **'Strip lights'**, **'Cyc strips'** (NA)

EXTRA TIPS

■ Install glass filters with the coated side towards the lamp as the dichroic coating reflects the unwanted wavelengths of light
■ 117 Steel Blue removes the warm tints produced when dimming a tungsten lamp source and it helps to maintain a whiter light
■ Always use a colour frame to hold a filter as it will start to buckle when it becomes very hot and reaches the point of plasticity
■ Darker/saturated colour filters create more heat and the level of light transmitted by the lantern is reduced

Extras!

8 COLOUR FILTERS

Extra resources – go to

www.leefilters.com – LEE Quick Start Videos; 'How Colour Works', 'Using Filters with LED'

www.leefilters.com – 'Resources' – 'Lighting Resources' – **'Think LEE'** provides a comprehensive guide to LEE products and a listing of filters in their colour order with a description of colour and suggestion for use to assist when selecting colours. There are spectral charts that fold out on the side with illustrative SPD curves for all colour samples, making it possible to check the wavelength transmission factors when selecting a colour from the main listing.

www.rosco.com – 'Colour Resource Gallery' and 'Masters of Stage Lighting and their ideas of Colour'

'An excellent design resource when planning the colour for a show'

Extra resources – go to

- ■ LEE Filters: www.leefilters.com
- ■ Roscolab: www.rosco.com
- ■ Apollo Design Technology: www.apollodesign.net/Products/View/3242.aspx

Colour packs available:

- ■ LEE Filters colour MAGIC – 'Series of eight individual packs each containing a selection of 12 filters 250mm x 300mm that relate to a particular aspect of lighting. Offers an opportunity to get to know the performance of various colour filters on offer in a cost effective way.' E.g. original, saturates, tint, complementary and light tint packs[11]
- ■ Roscolab – Colour Effects Kit – 12 30cm x 30cm filters, one of each colour, e.g. Cool/Warm, Saturated Colours, Diffusion[12]
- ■ The Apollo Apprentice Gel Kit – 'The purpose of the Apollo Apprentice Gel Kit is to train and educate. It simplifies the color selection process for beginning students, educators in lighting programs, and theater and architectural consultants.' Kit includes: 75 20" x 24" sheets (3 sheets of 25 colours), Apollo Gel Pen, Resource CD, Apollo Gel Swatchbook[13]

[11] LEE Filters – The Art of Colour
[12] Rosco – Product Catalogue
[13] Apollo Design inc website

Points for action

Quickies!

- Log on to www.leefilters.com: Click on Resources/Lighting Resources/ scroll down to Brochures and information/click on **'Think LEE'**
- **www.leefilters.com** – **Click on** 'Light' – 'Colour filters' – scroll down to 'LEE Filters Quick Start Videos' – **'How Colour Works'**: Lighting Designer Declan Randall Introduces the core principles of light and colour for lighting designers – **'Using Filters with LED'**: Lighting Designer Declan Randall Demonstrates the new LEE LED Filters
- Observe the effect of dimming a tungsten halogen lamp and the change in colour temperature
- Compare the transmission wavelengths of some commonly used colours by using the spectral charts in 'The Art of Colour'

A proper job!

- Set up three lanterns and try mixing primary and secondary colours to produce white light and observe the intermediate colours that can be created
- Try out the effect of a range of colour filters on skin tones and coloured materials

9 Gobos

A quick start – Using gobos

An introduction to working with metal and glass gobos

More info – Projecting and using images

Using gobos to create elements of scenery, add an atmosphere or dramatic effect

Extras! – Other types of gobos

Introducing dichroic break-ups, textured and coloured glass gobos

A quick start – Using gobos

Gobos provide the simplest form of projection and they can be used to create endless effects. An image or pattern can be projected by a Profile lantern by inserting a gobo into the centre of the optical system.

Two types of image projection gobos

- **Stainless steel** – a thin disc of stainless steel having a pattern etched through the surface; fine details of images have to be tagged in order to hold the pattern together. There is an extensive range of ready-made gobos available but custom steel gobos can be made to order from original artwork
- **Glass** – monochrome, black and white photographic or intricate geometric images can be etched on to glass discs. It is possible to project fine details as well as the effect of allowing light around a dark 'island' of image without the need to tag as with the steel gobos. Custom coloured gobos can be made to order. Glass gobos have a far longer life but are much more expensive than stainless steel; therefore, they are mainly used for long-running shows

Steel gobo – GMSL

Glass gobo – Roscolab

A quick start

9 GOBOS

Working with gobos

Gobos are mounted in gobo holders and inserted into the gate or iris slot of a Profile lantern:

- **The size of the gobo holder** must fit the make of lantern so it is important to check out the manufacturer's information as they all use different sizes; see below
- **The size of the gobo** must match the size of the gobo holder that fits the lantern. The three most common sizes used with generic lanterns are **'A'**, **'B'** & **'M'**

Lantern	Gobo Holder	Gobo Size
Altman – Shakespeare	GH09	B
ADB – Europe Series	GH34	A
CCT – Silhouette	GH01	A
ETC – Source Four	GH61	A
	GH59	B
Robert Juliat	GH58	B
Selecon – Acclaim Axial	GH60	M
Selecon	SPXGHB	B
Selecon – Pacific	GH72	A
Strand – SL	GH46	M

- **Set the lantern to produce a 'flat field'** with equal light distribution across the beam by adjusting the position of the lamp on the lamp tray, see Chapter 2 'Lanterns – performance luminaires – Extras! – Axial Ellipsoidal Profile'
- **Mount the gobo upside down and back to front** with the front side of the image facing the gobo holder. The optical system of the lantern inverts the image the right way up when it is projected
- **Insert the gobo holder into the guides at the rear of the gate slot** with the small raised clips holding the gobo facing the front of the lantern. If the holder is loose in the gate slot, you will be unable to accurately focus the gobo
- **The angle of the image** can be adjusted to compensate for the angle of projection of the lantern. This can be done by removing the gobo holder from the gate of the lantern and rotating the position of the circular gobo. Take care as the gobo will be very hot and gloves should be used or asbestos fingers!

Gobo in holder – GMSL

- **Circular-shaped holders** are produced by some lantern manufacturers which allow a degree of rotational adjustment without having to rotate the gobo disc
- **Rotating lens tubes** – The ETC Source Four and Selecon SPX and Pacific lanterns have a combination gate and lens tube that can be rotated. On the Strand SL the whole body of the lantern rotates within a circular yoke that is attached to the stirrup hanging bracket. The ADB Warp Profile also has a rotating gate feature
- **Using glass gobos** – the manufacturers provide strict guidelines for the use and handling of glass gobos, particularly with respect to adjusting the position of the lamp and lamp tray in the lantern being used

Types of gobo images - there are in excess of over 2,000 gobos available

Gobos can be grouped together under the following headings:

➤ **Realistic projected patterns**
Boundaries, Clouds, Occasions & Entertainment, Trees & Flowers, The World Around Us, Churches & Heraldics, Fire & Ice, Water, Windows Doors & Blinds, Wildlife, Sky

➤ **Non-realistic patterns**
Abstract, Break-ups, Foliage break-ups, Graphics & Grills, Rotation

➤ **Graphics**
Architecture & Retail, Graphics, Text

Realistic gobo –
Roscolab

Leaf break-up –
Roscolab

Ritz gobo –
Roscolab

Did you know that –
- The 'Tadpole' is a customised gobo holder that can be rotated by its long tail that is designed to stay cool to touch and can be secured in the final adjusted position
- **'Goes Before Optics'** is a derivation of the term gobo which is a term used in the motion-picture industry where 'flags' or 'cookies' are placed in the beam of a light source to create shadows[14]

[14] Wikipedia, the free encyclopedia

9 GOBOS **A quick start**

More info

9 GOBOS

Naturally occurring sources of light

An intense source of light produces the effects of shadows as can been seen when using a follow spot. Sun and moonlight produce naturally occurring patterns of light and shade that can be introduced into lighting a scene to break down a flat wash of light and add interest to the lighting.

Lighting in a room

Strong sunlight shining through a window casts a brightly shaped area of light on to the floor or walls of a room, projecting the pattern of the window bars. Similar effects are created as the outside light passes through vertical bars or horizontal Venetian blinds.

These effects can be created on-stage by focusing off-stage lanterns through the window of the set to project a natural shadow or they can be simulated by projecting a gobo pattern from an overhead lantern. The mood, time of day or the change of the effects of the weather can be achieved by subtle changes in the length and position of the shadows and colour of the light.

Scenic projections using realistic patterns

A window effect can be created by projecting a gobo on to a small suspended rectangular screen with the pattern of light passing through the window being projected on to the stage from a second gobo to heighten the effect.

➤ **A window gobo** will add depth to the setting and it can also:

Window gobo – GMSL

- suggest the period of the setting – medieval church, Georgian, eastern or modern window – and it can dramatically change the type of room depending upon the shape, style and angle of projection of the window along with the ambient light
- suggest the changes in time of day by a change of colour, e.g. bright sunlight coming through a shuttered window or moonlight through prison bars
- show the effect of the outside light coming into the room and the shadow that is cast by the light passing through the window

➤ The following effects can be produced by using window gobos and up to four Profile lanterns:

- **Change in the time of day** – crossfade two Profile lanterns projecting the same window bar gobo accurately overlaid on top of each other, each having different colours, one suggesting day, the other night

- **The light coming through the window** – position a Profile lantern with the same window bar gobo to project on to the floor from behind the hanging window projected image
- **Lightning effect** – project a forked lightning gobo on to the window effect with a night-time colour. The lightning can be enhanced by flashing the floor window pattern with the lightning. Remember that we see the lightning before we hear the thunder as light travels faster than sound

Lightning gobo – GMSL

➤ **A stained glass window projection** will immediately create the atmosphere of being in a church; add some organ music and you can create the full effect. The projected gobo will require a break-up of coloured light which can be achieved either by using a split/broken colour filter or a Prismatic gobo; see 'Extras!'

The above effects can be viewed on the 'Online video link – 9.1 Using Gobos' see page 157.

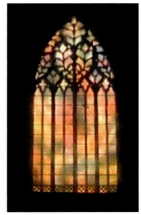

Stained glass window – GMSL

9 GOBOS   More info

Light outside

Direct sunlight casts the shadows of building and other objects on to the ground. It is also broken up by branches and tree foliage and reflected by water. Firelight creates moving patterns. These effects can be created on-stage by using break-ups and patterned gobos from lanterns on to the stage surface, scenery or costumes.

Abstract projections using non-realistic patterns

➤ **Forest and woodland effects**
There are various foliage/leaf break-ups that can be used to create bright shafts of sunlight in a dense forest or the dappled effect of light passing

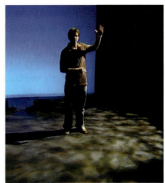

Leaf break-up – GMSL

through woodland foliage. The shafts of sunlight may be projected from overhead or perhaps more dramatically as back or side lighting. As the actors pass through the wash of dappled downlighting, their faces and costumes will be picked up alternately by the coloured highlights and shadows.

159

EXTRA TIPS

- Make sure that the steel gobo is mounted in the front of the universal iris slot holder on the lens side of the lantern when combined with a Prismatic or Colorizer gobo so that the image can be accurately focused
- See the Rosco Product Catalogue for some excellent photographs showing the use of dichroic break-ups and glass gobos
- There are some good video clips on the Apollo Design Technology website showing how to mount gobos and insert them in the lanterns

Extra resources – go to

www.rosco.com –   Rosco Product catalogue, examples of using Colorizers, Prismatics, Image Glass & ColorWaves
www.rosco.com –   DHA Rosco Gobo Catalogue
www.apollodesign.net /products/dichroics – Apollo Design Technology
www.apollodesign.net –   The Apollo Gobo Tool Kit –

'The purpose of the Apollo Gobo Tool Kit is to train and educate. It introduces the basics of using gobos to create visual effects in general stage lighting applications.' Kit includes: Apollo SuperHolder, Creative Effects Guide, Instructional DVD, Resource DVD, (24) B-Round Metal Standards, B-Round B&W Glass Standard

Points for action

Quickies!

- Look at the different types of Colorizers, Prismatics, Image Glass & ColorWaves and examples of their use either on the Rosco website or in the Rosco Product Guide
- Obtain a copy of the Rosco Product Guide

10 Motion effects

A quick start – Animation, rotating gobos & projections

Introducing the use of animation discs, rotating gobos and projections

More info – Animation & rotator effects

Comparing the range of effects that are available on animation discs and gobo rotators

Extras! – Using the three types of rotators to create effects

Creating gobo effects and looking at three different types of rotators and the manufacturers' variations

A quick start – Animation, rotating gobos & projections

Moving effects can be used to create a theatrical illusion and add an extra dimension to a scene. Effects can be achieved by breaking up the beam of light projected from a lantern with a rotating disc or by rotating a gobo image. Realistic moving images like clouds, rain and snow can also be projected by an optical projector.

Animation discs

Animation discs are simple to use and they provide a low-cost method of producing moving lighting effects. An etched metal disc powered by an electric motor unit is mounted in the colour frame holder of the lantern. The slow-turning disc breaks up the beam of light, creating an illusion of movement. The motor unit has an onboard direction and variable speed controls allowing it to be powered direct from an independent power supply or from a dimmer circuit to provide a remote speed control.

➤ **Moving shadow effects**
Flickering effect similar to the reflected light from a fire or water can be created with a Coarse Radial or Tangential animation disc mounted in front of a PC, Fresnel or Parcan. These lanterns provide a wide beam of light but they project

a very basic direct image which needs to be softened by adding a light frost with the colour filter in the colour frame slot.

➤ Adding movement to projected images

Animation discs can add movement to static gobo images projected by Profiles and Ellipsoidal lanterns. They can convert a projected flames gobo into a burning fire, create moving clouds, falling snow, rain and rippling water. The gobo can be independently focused as the animation disc rotates in front of the lantern and its optical system. The effect can be enhanced by adding split colours in the rear of the colour frame runners or by attaching colours to the rotating disc. 'The key to the system is to choose the right gobo for the base effect.'[18]

Animation disc – Roscolab

➤ Direction of movement

The direction of the movement can be changed by adjusting the position of the motor in the front of the lens tube:

- Side to side – mount the motor position above the lens tube
- Up and down – mount the motor position at the side of the lens tube

➤ Focus and speed

For maximum effect, the gobo should be focused between hard and soft focus:

- Hard focus produces minimal movement and the animation hardly works
- Soft focus produces maximum movement but the gobo pattern is lost
- The animated movement is dependent on the speed of the disc and the type of gobo selected

Gobo rotators

Motion effects can be created by rotating a single or double gobo in the path of the light from a Profile lantern. A whole range of abstract and dramatic effects can be achieved depending upon the choice of gobos, speed, direction of the rotation and the use of other static, textured or coloured gobos in the gobo slot. Add some smoke and colour and some vibrant moving effects can be created.

Rotator drive units

The gobo is mounted in a motorised drive unit that accurately rotates on the central axis of a profile lantern. The unit is inserted into the iris slot in the gate of the lantern, allowing the addition of a standard static gobo holder to be accommodated. A rotator

---

[18] Guide to Motion Effects Rosco

unit can take either one or two gobos that can be independently driven in opposite directions at selected speeds.

> **Power and control**
> Stand-alone rotators are powered directly from an external mains socket having on-board speed and direction controls.

Vortex rotator – Roscolab

Two sizes of gobo rotator units

> **Standard 'B'-size gobo rotator units:**
> - **Gobos** – suitable for use with metal or glass gobos or any combination of Colorizer, Prismatics, Image Glass and Colour Waves
> - **Lanterns** – 'B'-size gobo rotators will fit ETC Source Four, Strand SL, Altman Shakespeare, Philips Selecon SPX & Pacific; CCT Silhouette, Project & Freedom

> **'M'-size gobo single rotator unit** – Apollo 'Smart Move Jr'
> - **Gobos** – only suitable for use with metal or glass gobos
> - **Lanterns** – 'M'-size gobo rotators will fit ETC Source Four Junior, Philips Selecon Acclaim

Projected effects

Moving visual effects can be produced using an optical effects disc with an effects projector:

- The effects projector uses a powerful lamp 2000W/2500W and a high-quality optical system to provide an exceptional light output. Plates can be used to mask off areas of the projection and beam diverters to project the image through 90 degrees on to the stage[19]
- The optical effects disc unit consists of a rotating etched glass disc and motor contained in a metal casing with an objective lens mounted on the front
- The disc unit is fixed in front of the projector housing so that the effects disc rotates through the focus point of the lantern's optical system. The speed and direction can be controlled by the onboard controls or by DMX

Effects projector – Stage Electrics

[19] The Hire Store – Stage Electrics

10 MOTION EFFECTS   A quick start

A quick start

11 PROJECTED IMAGES

Using the slides

- The acetate slides should be mounted in a Selecon heat-reducing slide holder
- Mount the slide upside down in between the UV heat-reducing filter and the glass cover
- The viewing side of the slide should be facing the thick UV filter in the slide holder
- Insert the slide holder in the iris slot in the gate with the UV filter facing the lamp source and the glass cover facing the front of the lantern

Selecon slide holder – GMSL

MORE TIPS

- An acetate slide can melt in front of your eyes if the lantern isn't correctly set up or a laser print is mounted the wrong way round so be sure to make some duplicate copies

More resources – go to

www.seleconlight.com: Click on resources/scroll down to Technical Support – Information on making and using plastic slides

Points for action

Quickies!

- Investigate making plastic images on the Selecon website

More info – Projecting digital images

Digital projection can be used to project high-quality still or moving images that can be integrated as a part of a production.

Digital projection

Digital images can projected by connecting a digital projector to laptop running Microsoft Powerpoint. Digital content, still images, photographs, graphics or video content can be downloaded to build up a sequence which can be used for college or small productions. It can be used to create the set and it allows scene changes to happen instantly without the need of full sized sets that can be expensive to construct and take up a large amount of wing space.

Using digital images

There are a variety of ways that computer-generated or video images can be used to provide virtual reality backdrops, abstracted moving video images, projected images, captions for documentary drama, integrated moving images or effects projected on to the stage. The possibilities are endless but the problem is of creating a seamless integration of the images and effects as a part of the production so that they are developed naturally from the text and drama or a part of choreographed dance or movement.

Projected imagery needs to be a part of the overall design concept and not a bolt-on technical spectacle to add a 'wow' factor to the production. Theatre has different requirements to film or television and therefore video material needs to be specially prepared with this in mind to enhance and blend with the requirements of the production, unless documentary-type material is required.

'There is only one right way to design a play by respecting the text, and not using it as a peg on which to advertise your skills, whatever they may be, nor to work out your psychological hang-ups with some fashionable gimmick.' Jocelyn Herbert, theatre designer[26]

Using digital projection

There are three areas that need to be considered:

➤ **Where is the image to be projected?**
  - An area of the set specifically designed to take the projection
  - An existing vertical surface rear wall painted white or backcloth
  - A commercial projection screen either suspended or incorporated into the set
  - The stage floor where this is in view of the audience
  - On to moving or static bodies, textured or coloured walls, or other objects either large or small

[26] Designers on Colour – Roscolab Guide to Colour Filters

➤ **Reflectivity of the projection surface**

Commercial screen material will have a higher level of reflection than a white painted surface and therefore produce a brighter image. The reflectivity on the surface of a back projection screen can be reduced depending upon the type of materials being used. Grey screens provide a wider viewing angle than black.

➤ **Projector**

The light output of the projector which is measured in lumens affects the brightness of projected image:

- 3000/3500 lumens projector may be suitable for a small to medium space depending upon the amount of ambient/reflected light falling on the screen
- 6500 lumens projector provides a higher light output
- The size of the image and the distance of the projector from the screen will affect the brightness of the image
- As a guide, the standard lens requires the projector to be positioned twice as far from the screen as the width of the projected image
- Interchangeable long throw or wide-angled lenses are available for some projectors

➤ **Front projection**

There are a number of things to consider when positioning the projector in front of the actors:

- When projecting on to large surfaces, the image may spill on to the actors' faces and bodies and can create quite a surrealistic effect depending upon the image. This can enhance or detract from the action depending upon the requirements of the production
- Projection overspill on to the actors can be balanced out by increasing the front lighting but there is a danger of it washing out the projection
- Projecting above head level providing there is sufficient height will remove the overspill on to the actors. However, the set may need to be extended to fill in the lower vertical area across the stage
- Increasing the angle of projection by mounting the projector overhead on a front lighting bar allows the image to be projected starting at floor level. The overspill on to the actors will now only occur at the rear of the stage creating an up stage 'no go' area and lost acting space
- A 'key stone' effect occurs when projecting on to a screen from an angle and this can be adjusted via the menu function of the projector. Key stone adjustment is a bit like using the shutters on a Profile spot except the shape of the projected image is adjusted rather than the beam being shaped. Zoom facilities are also available allowing the size of the image to be adjusted to fit the screen. Computer images can be reshaped and masked to prevent overspill when projecting on to non-standard-format-sized screens

➤ Rear projection

Positioning the projector behind the actors to project on to a rear projection screen removes the problem of actors walking through the projected image but there are other considerations:

- The position of the projector and screen will reduce the acting space so this is only possible on a deep stage
- A projector with a wide-angle lens will reduce the depth required for projection
- A special screen made up of back projection material will be required; this could be made as a part of the set or hired depending upon the size required
- The audience views the image from the reverse side but it is possible to reverse this on some projectors and it can also be done on the computer

➤ Controlling the images

- Microsoft PowerPoint can be used as a basic program to build up slide sequences of pictures, text, graphics, video animation and audio
- Rosco Keystroke provides an interface for video playback programs, PowerPoint, Keynote, Quicktime or Windows Media Player and sound playback programs including ProTools, iTunes, Garageband and SFX

MORE TIPS

- 'Front White' screens are used for front projection
- 'Twin White' screens can be used for front or rear projection with no apparent difference in picture brightness
- 'Grey' screens are used for back projection. They provide a neutral-coloured background and have a wider viewing angle
- 'Black' screens are used when there is high ambient light, providing fine detailed resolution when back lit with a strong image[27]
- 'Black' screens have the narrowest viewing angle, that is the reduction in the quality of the image when viewed from the side

---

[27] Rosco Product Catalogue

11 PROJECTED IMAGES   **More info**

An example of a transformation

➤ *Swan Lake* **ballet** – Director/Choreographer Mathew Bourne, New Adventures & Backrow Productions
Designer Lez Brotherston, Lighting design Rick Fisher, Photographer Mike Rothwell

'This was a very traditional gauze (or as referred to in the US scrim) dissolve. The gauze was a painted, sharkstooth gauze and there was a separately flown black cloth on the bar immediately upstage of it.' Rick Fisher, Lighting designer

Swan Lake – *New Adventures & Backrow Productions – Lighting Design Rick Fisher, Photographer Mike Rothwell*

'Front cloth scene of the billboard outside the nightclub'

'In the front gauze scene there was some front light from the balcony profiles or fresnels depending on the distance shaped to the full stage size of the gauze, supplemented by some carefully focused lights that scrape down the cloth and highlight specific parts of the painting of the gauze.' Rick Fisher, Lighting designer

Swan Lake – *New Adventures & Backrow Productions – Lighting Design Rick Fisher, Photographer Mike Rothwell*

'As the main characters pass through the door into the nightclub'

'Then on cue the lighting is changed, the lights on the front of the painted drop are taken out as the black backing cloth is flown out to reveal the silhouette of the dancers upstage, where the light is carefully focused to not light the gauze itself, and then finally the light builds as the gauze is flown out allowing the dancers to fill the stage space.'

Rick Fisher, Lighting designer

Swan Lake *club scene – Mike Rothwell*

13 OTHER EFFECTS   More info

Lighting the Performance Space

Getting started – Looking at different angles of lighting, how they affect the illumination of the face and body when used to light a performance space for drama, dance and musical theatre. Also looking at creating a lighting palette and applying the elements and tools of lighting to lighting a show.

14 Angles of illumination

A quick start – Source & direction of light

Looking at the effects of the direction and angle of light on the face and body

More info – Front lighting

Planning a grid of lighting areas to provide a wash of light

Extras! – Creating a wash of light

Setting up a flat frontal and cross area lighting grid

A quick start – Source & direction of light

The direction, height and angle of the sources of light produce different effects of illumination. The performer on-stage can be lit from an all-round angle of 360 degrees.

 Online video link – 14.1 Angles of illumination
https://vimeo.com/123717962

Experimenting with a source of light

Take a single source of light and move its position over the head, face and body first from front to back and then from side to side and see how it changes and affects the illumination. You can try this out with a torch, desk light or a lantern mounted on a stand.

GMSL

- **Vertical overhead beam:** This produces a tight pool of light highlighting the nose but the eyes and mouth remain in shadow. It creates a very dramatic effect but the light doesn't fully illuminate the features of the face when viewed from the front

GMSL

- **Angled beam from behind:** If the source of light is moved behind, it throws the body into shadow, creating a silhouette and halo effect around the head. The face cannot be seen and a shadow of the body is cast in front of the subject

GMSL

- **Front angled beam:** As the source of light is moved forward in front of the subject, the shadows under the eyes and mouth are reduced. At an overhead angle of 45 degrees, the features of the face are well lit. As the source is lowered, the light spreads backwards and the shadow of the head and body increases

GMSL

- **Front horizontal beam:** When the beam is directly in front of and level with the face, it flattens out the features and produces a large shadow of the body

GMSL

- **Side horizontal beam:** If the horizontal source is moved around to the side of the subject, it will highlight the features of the side of the face and profile the shoulders and body. The shadow is now cast to the side and is less obvious when viewed from the front

GMSL

- **Front low beam:** A low beam of light from the front illuminates under the chin and the eyes that would normally be in shadow from overhead lighting. A low source on its own tends to distort the features of the face, creating a dramatic effect and the size of the shadow is increased, making it larger than life. When used with overhead lighting, it can provide a useful fill light. Footlights used to create a similar effect but they are now not generally used (see 'Did you know that'). Par 16 Birdies are used to create a similar but more controlled effect

GMSL

- **Side low beam:** If the low beam of light is moved to the side, it will provide an alternative angle of floor lighting illumination, profiling the features of the head and body

14. ANGLES OF ILLUMINATION   A quick start

 Online video link – 14.2 Three angles of lighting
https://vimeo.com/123717963

Lighting the face

For drama it is important to be able to see the facial expressions; being able to see the mouth also assists the audience's ability to hear the actor clearly.

- **Overhead angle of 45 degrees** from the front provides good illumination of the face and upper body, reducing the shadow cast

GMSL

- **Single source of illumination** overhead directly from the front at an angle of 45 degrees produces a tight area of light, reducing the shadow cast by the body. The illumination and profiling of the face tends to be flat; note the single shadow under the chin

GMSL

- **Two sources of illumination** positioned at an overhead angle of 45 degrees and at a horizontal angle of 45 degrees either side of the subject spread the light, increasing the shadows of the body cast sideways

The illumination and profiling of the face is increased and the shadows either side of the nose are reduced; note the lighter double shadow under the chin

GMSL

A quick start

14 ANGLES OF ILLUMINATION

Three directions of lighting

The stage is illuminated from a range of directions and positions from overhead, the side and from behind.

➤ **Front lighting:**
   This is the main source of illumination for the action, being angled to illuminate the face for drama or directly overhead to light the body for dance.

➤ **Side lighting:**
   This is a secondary source of lighting used to profile the face and body, illuminating the shoulders and the sides of the face. It removes the shadows created by front lighting and illuminates the moving body for dance. It is used at three different positions: floor, head and high-level cross lighting diagonally across the stage.

➤ **Back lighting:**
   This is another secondary light source from behind, it adds depth to the scene by highlighting the head and shoulders. It creates a dramatic shadow-like effect, making the actor stand out from the background.

The different directions and angles of illumination can be combined when lighting the stage to light the face and body or to create special effects.

Points for action

Takes longer
■ Experiment with a source of light to try out the effects as above. You could use a portable light source and a polystyrene head block. If you use a lantern, take care as it will become hot and the lamp can be damaged when it is moved, as the filament is very fragile when burning or when it is still hot

A proper job!
■ Use three lanterns to light an area with a single source and two sources of illumination and compare the difference

14. ANGLES OF ILLUMINATION   A quick start

More info – Front lighting

Front lighting provides the main source of illumination for a performance space. A basic requirement is to be able to light the whole space with an even wash of light. This can be achieved by the careful blending of a series of lighting areas produced by a multiple of lanterns/luminaires.

Creating a wash of light

A wash of light can be created by dividing the performance space into a grid of lighting areas that can be blended together to provide the same quality of light across the space. If the lanterns lighting each area are controlled by separate dimmers, then they can be selected individually to create smaller areas. If the width of the space is divided into an odd number of areas, it will provide a central area which is frequently an important focus for drama that needs to be lit separately.

➤ **Planning a grid of areas**
It is easier to work out a simple plan on paper before starting to hang the lanterns. You will need a lighting layout plan of the space with lighting bars and the positions and circuit numbers of the outlet sockets marked on it. Initially, you may find it easier to plan the position of the areas and positions of the lanterns by walking the stage but with experience you will be able to draw it directly on to the plan.

- **Centre stage** is an essential area and so there will be an odd number of areas across the stage
- **A small stage** or drama studio can be divided up into six lighting areas, three across by two deep
- **A deeper stage** may require an additional row of areas dividing it up into nine lighting areas
- **A wider stage** may need to be divided into five areas across

In a studio or on a small stage, the lighting bars may be hung in a fixed position. To provide an even cover of light from front to back, the lanterns on the first bar need to light the areas positioned immediately under the next lighting bar up stage.[1] The lanterns from the second bar will need to light the areas under the next bar, with the beams crossing over above head height to provide an even cover up and down stage between the two rows of areas. With fixed bars, it may not be possible to maintain a front overhead angle of 45 degrees.

On a larger stage where there is a suspension grid, the position and height of the bars can be adjusted to maintain the optimum angle of illumination when lighting the areas. The positions of the bars can be planned on a side elevation drawing of the stage to provide an overhead angle of illumination of 45 degrees, with the beams crossing over up and down stage above head height to provide a smooth wash.[2]

[1] See 'Angles of illumination – Extras! – Navigating the stage'
[2] See the side elevation drawing on page 200

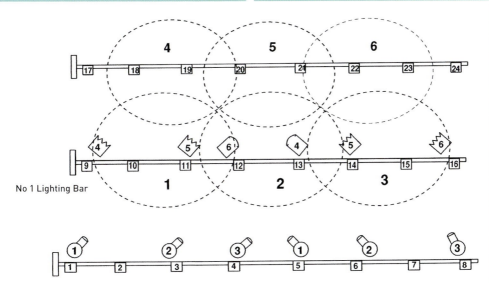

No 1 Lighting Bar

F.O.H. Front of House

Six-area lighting plan – GMSL

- **Planning the areas** – it is easier to walk across the stage to visualise the positions of the lighting areas
- **Draw in the positions** of the areas on the plan, i.e. the positions where the actors will be standing and their faces lit by the beam of light. This is not the position where the beam will hit the floor as this will be behind the lighting area. See the side elevation drawing on page 200
- **Number the areas** in a logical sequence, front line across 1, 2, 3 as viewed by the audience from House Left to House Right (Stage Right to Stage Left) and the second line of areas 4, 5, 6 as on the plan above
- **A logical sequence of numbering** from 'House Left' to 'House Right' and from front to back will make it easier to remember the area numbers when viewing the stage from the front and directing the lighting or operating the control desk

14 ANGLES OF ILLUMINATION   **More info**

Connecting the lanterns to the dimmers & control

The lanterns are connected via the circuit outlet sockets to the dimmer units and control channel faders on the lighting desk.

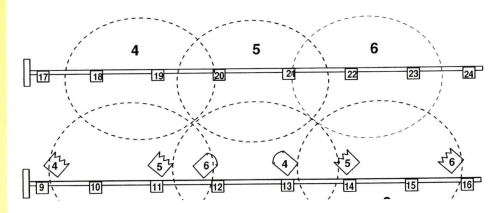

Three-area lighting plan – GMSL

➤ **On the lantern plan**
- **Number each lantern symbol** with the same number as the area that it is lighting
- **For an example** see the above plan:

    Area 4 is lit by two lanterns numbered No.4 connected to outlet circuits Nos. 9 & 13

    Area 5 is lit by two lanterns numbered No.5 connected to outlet circuits Nos. 11 & 14

    Area 6 is lit by two lanterns numbered No.6 connected to outlet circuits Nos. 12 & 16

➤ **Hard patching system with dimmer packs**
On a system with hard patching, the lanterns are connected via a cable patch to the dimmer packs. They can be individually hard patched to the dimmer units so that the lanterns are controlled by the same channel fader number on the lighting desk as the area that they are lighting in the following way:

6-Way Dimmer Pack

Dimmer channel Nos.	1	2	3	4	5	6	
Two outlet sockets per dimmer channel (paired)				9	11	12	Outlet circuit numbers patched to dimmer channels
				13	14	16	

14 ANGLES OF ILLUMINATION **More info**

- The lanterns lighting area 4 are connected via outlet circuits Nos.9 & 13
- Outlet circuits Nos.9 & 13 are patched to dimmer No.4 which is controlled by channel fader No.4 below
- The lanterns lighting area 4 will now be controlled by channel fader No.4, providing the lighting control desk has been set with a 1:1 soft patch

Hardwired systems with dimmer racks

On a hardwired system, the lanterns are connected via the outlet circuits directly to the dimmer rack. If the lighting desk is set to a 1:1 soft patch, they are controlled by the same channel fader number as the circuit outlet socket number that the lantern is connected to.

The control channel faders on an advanced memory lighting desk can be soft patched or assigned to any of the dimmer units in the rack. The lanterns are controlled by the same channel fader number on the lighting desk as the area that they are lighting in the following way:

- The lanterns lighting area 4 are connected via outlet circuits to the dimmer units Nos.9 & 13 which have the same DMX address numbers
- Control channel fader No.4 is programmed and assigned to the DMX addresses 9 & 13
- The lanterns lighting area 4 will now be controlled by channel fader No.4 [3] [4]

Soft Patching	
Control Channel Fader No.	Dimmer DMX Address No.
4	9 & 13
5	11 & 13
6	12 &16

QUICK TIPS

- Lay out the lanterns on the stage directly under the position on the bar where they are to be hung. This is a practical way to plan the distribution of your lanterns
- Check that the lanterns are positioned symmetrically either side of the centre of the bar and up and down stage before hanging them, in order to produce matching angles and an even wash of light

[3] See Chapter 5 'Lighting controls – Extras! – Soft patching'
[4] See Chapter 20 'The design process – Extras! – Patching/hook-up schedule'

Cross area Lighting

➤ **Six-area front view**

On the opposite page, the front view of the stage shows the beams from the three lanterns on each bar overlapping above head height across the stage and from front to back to provide a seamless wash.

- The actor standing in area 1 is illuminated by two lanterns lighting down stage right
- As the actor moves towards area 2, they should walk into the beams of light from the pair of lanterns lighting the down stage centre area and on into the beams of light lighting area 3

> **❯ Online video link – 14.4 Cross area lighting**
> https://vimeo.com/123717965

➤ **Six-area lighting plan**

On the plan, the lighting areas are lit in the following way:

- **Down stage areas 1, 2 & 3**
  FOH advance bar in front of the stage 6 x Profile spots, two lanterns per area
  Area 2 centre stage is lit by two lanterns numbered No.2 positioned at an angle of 45 degrees either side of the area making a combined horizontal angle of 90 degrees
  Areas 1 & 3 left and right, one lantern is positioned at the extreme off-stage end of the lighting bar and the other is positioned on the opposite side of the centre of the bar, maintaining a combined angle of 90 degrees. Therefore, the beams of light from the two lanterns either side of centre cross over to light areas 1 & 3. If an advance bar is not available, the areas would be lit by cross area lighting using Profile spots positioned on the sides of the auditorium

- **Centre stage areas 4, 5 & 6**
  No.1 lighting bar over stage, Lx1. 2 x PC, 4 x Fresnel lanterns with barndoors, two lanterns per area
  Area 5 centre stage is lit by two Fresnels numbered No.5 positioned at a combined angle of 90 degrees to the centre of the area
  Areas 4 & 6 left & right – Fresnel lantern is positioned at the extreme off-stage end of the lighting bar and a PC is positioned just on the other side of the centre of the bar, maintaining a combined angle of 90 degrees. The Fresnels are used to light the extreme off-stage side areas because of their wide spread over a short distance. The PCs are positioned on the opposite side of the centre of the bar. They are used in preference to a Fresnel as they have a longer throw and a tighter beam, reducing the scatter light on the side of the stage. If PCs are not available, Fresnels can be used but barndoors are essential to contain the spill of light

- **Patching** – note from the plan that the two lanterns lighting each area are paired together so that they are controlled by the same channel control fader

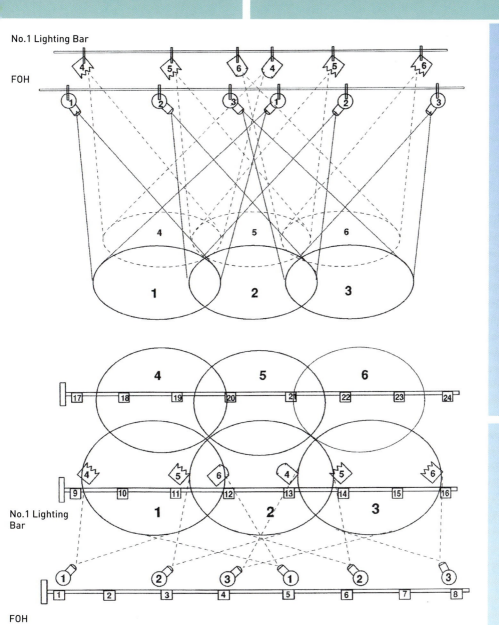

No.1 Lighting Bar

FOH

No.1 Lighting Bar

FOH

Cross area lighting plan and elevation – GMSL

Navigating the stage

The stage can be conveniently divided into a grid of areas and standard directions that are useful when directing lighting and for the position of lighting areas. They are primarily used to direct the movement of the actors by the director when facing the action from the front and for the stage manager to record or 'block' the moves.

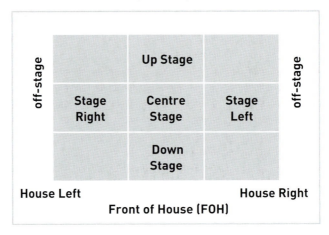

- **Stage left SL & Stage right SR** – actors left and right when facing the audience
- **Centre stage CS** – in the middle
- **Up & down stage US, DS** – away from the audience and towards the audience
- **On- & off-stage** – towards centre stage and away from the centre
- **Front of House (FOH)** – the area in front of the stage used by the audience
- **House left & right** – left and right of auditorium as viewed by the audience

More information on the complete grid of areas can be found in 'Lighting jargon'.

Did you know that –

- The stage directions were devised so that the director could easily direct the moves of the actors in rehearsal. Using stage left and right (the actors' left and right) removed any confusion of whether the instructions given were actors' left or the director's left!
- Up and down stage – this term dates back to when stages in theatre were built with a rake or slope. This was to work with the perspective scenery and also to raise the viewpoint of the actor up stage. Hence the term 'being upstaged' by another actor, causing the other actors to turn away from the audience
- It was said that Laurence Olivier, one of the UK's most famous actors, when playing Shakespeare's Richard III at the London Old Vic always limped with his up stage leg! The Old Vic had quite a steep rake

15 Other angles of lighting

A quick start – FOH lighting
FOH and cross side lighting

More info – Side, cross & back lighting
Floor, head, cross and back lighting

Extras! – Focusing a wash of light
Focusing the lanterns to create a wash of light

A quick start – FOH lighting

FOH lighting is a traditional term for the lanterns mounted in front of the proscenium arch lighting the front of the stage. In some halls or larger theatres, the lanterns are mounted on horizontal and vertical bars on the side walls of the auditorium. These positions provide alternative angles of lighting to an advance bar directly in front of the stage.

Height and angles of illumination

In many auditoriums it can be difficult to maintain the optimum angle of 45° to illuminate the face, as the angle of illumination may vary between 35° and 60°. In some theatres, an advance bar has been added in front of the proscenium to provide a suitable angle to light the front of the stage.

Side auditorium lighting

It is more difficult to maintain a near vertical angle of 45 degrees and to produce an even wash across the stage when the FOH lighting positions are on the side of the auditorium on horizontal bars or vertical booms. Therefore, it is important to use the lanterns in a specific order to try to maintain a steep angle and achieve the best results. In these positions, Profile spots need to be used to throw over a longer distance and it may be necessary to use Axial lanterns or larger-wattage Profiles to achieve an adequate level of illumination.

 Online video link – 15.1 Focusing lighting

➤ **Horizontal bars** mounted on the side wall
The beams of light from the three lanterns need to spread like a fan across the stage:

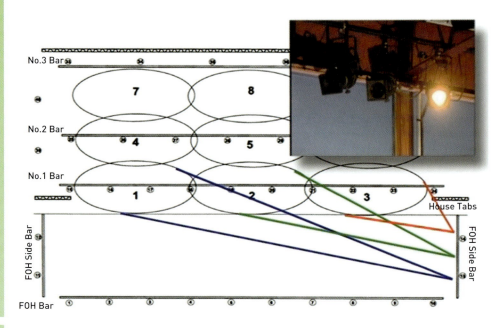

FOH lighting hung on horizontal bars – GMSL

- The lantern nearest to the stage is used to light the off-stage area on the same side
- The middle lantern is used to light the centre area
- The lantern positioned furthest away from the stage is used to light the opposite side

➤ **Vertical boom bars** mounted on the side wall

The beams of light from the three lanterns need to spread in a similar vertical fan pattern across the stage. They are used in the following order to endeavour to maintain the best possible angle of elevation:

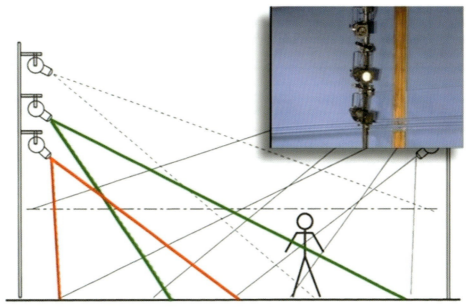

Front elevation of the stage

FOH lighting mounted on vertical booms – GMSL

- ■ The bottom lantern to cover the shortest distance to light the off-stage area on the same side
- ■ The middle lantern to light the centre area
- ■ The top lantern to cover the longest distance and to light the off-stage area on the opposite side

15 OTHER ANGLES OF LIGHTING

A quick start

War Horse – *National Theatre production – Lighting Design Paule Constable, Photograph © Simon Annand*

'The low-level back lighting captured on this picture cuts in at a shallow angle almost from the side, highlighting the profile of the men on horses.'

- Varying the height of the back lighting can heighten the dramatic effect as can be seen in the Royal National Theatre production of *War Horse*.

The effect of using layers of lighting

In the production of *War Horse*, Paule Constable uses the effect of different layers of back and side lighting to achieve two distinct looks and places in a space of darkness that is defined by light. The hell of the First World War zone is created using low dynamic angles of lighting from under the projection screen of harsh blue white light from discharge source lanterns of a man-made manufactured environment. (See illustrations Chapter 11 'Projected images – Extras!') This is contrasted with the high angles of warm beautiful sunlight for the rural Devon community scenes.[5]

[5] *The Making of War Horse*, More Four

Layers of FOH lighting

Modern theatres are designed with lighting bridges and slots over the auditorium and side boom positions within the architectural design. However the architecture of older theatres was not originally designed for the requirements of modern lighting. Originally in the early days of electric light the front of the stage was lit with the minimum of lanterns hung at the centre in front of the Dress or Upper circles that tended to produce a very flat wash of light.

With the ongoing programmes of refurbishment of theatre auditoriums, lighting positions have been improved as can be seen in the FOH positions at the Theatre Royal Bath built by C J Phipps 1863. A side lighting boom has been positioned in a specially created slip position behind the proscenium arch boxes. Cross side lighting positions have been set into the ceiling of the Dress circle and also a bar above in the Upper circle. Finally a high level central FOH bar has been added below the main auditorium ceiling above the Upper circle. These positions have removed the lanterns from obscuring the architectural plasterwork and also provided a range of varying angles and layers of light.

FOH lighting positions Theatre Royal Bath – Skip Mort

Layers of lighting as used on a thrust stage

A similar effect can be seen in the lighting positions for the thrust stage of the Royal Shakespeare Theatre and the RSC Swan. The three levels of generic lanterns, Source Four Profiles and Pars, surround the three sides of the courtyard style thrust stage providing a controlled wash of light. The lanterns are fitted with colour scroller units to provide instant change of colour and mood of the general lighting. The

Auditorium lighting RST – Photo by Peter Cook © RSC

239

16 The lighting palette

A quick start – A palette of lighting areas

Creating a palette of lighting areas for drama, dance and musical theatre

More info – A touch of colour

Looking at the effects of colour and exploring the use of the colour palette

Extras! – Adding colour

Techniques in using coloured lighting to create effects

A quick start – A palette of lighting areas

The lighting designer aims to create a palette of areas and angles of illumination that can be used to compose scenes of light.

Creating a lighting palette[7]

A grid of areas are planned based on the dramatic requirements of the production to light the main acting areas, solo areas, to provide accent and feature lighting, and broader washes of light.

> **Online video link – 16.1 The lighting palette**
> https://vimeo.com/123718047

➤ **Lighting for drama**
  The lighting palette for drama will depend upon whether it is an interior, exterior, realistic or abstract setting. When lighting a drama production, the main emphasis is to illuminate the face and body:

[7] Based on *Method of Lighting the Stage*, Stanley McCandless (1897–1967); also developed in *Lighting the Amateur Stage* by Francis Reid

245

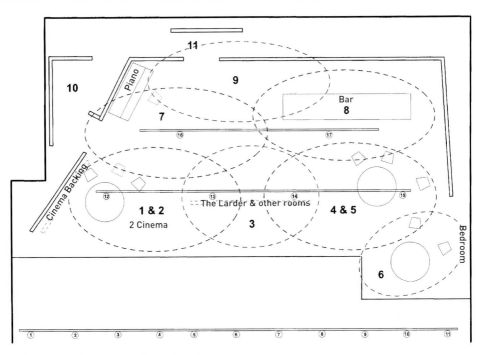

'Allo 'Allo *lighting area plan – Skip Mort*

- **The lighting areas** will be defined by the action. On an interior setting, the focus will be on the position of the furniture and also the entrances. For a small production, this may be based on a nine-area grid: three across and three deep. The areas may not be symmetrical and the size will depend upon the action. Each of the areas will need to overlap and be independently controlled to balance the intensities to produce a seamless wash or to focus the attention to suit the action
- **Specials** reproducing the ambient illumination from practical light fittings on the set
- **Flat frontal or cross area lighting** may be used to illuminate the areas. Direct frontal area lighting tends to be visually flat, and side, cross and back lighting will need to be added to provide highlights, specific natural or dramatic effects
- **Side head lighting** can be used to provide light from natural sources, sun or moonlight through a window, the low glow of a setting sun or from artificial sources through the door from another room, the side light from a candle or table light
- **Cross or back lighting** can provide the effect of high-level sunlight or moonlight; strong colours can be used in the back lighting to create moods without affecting the illumination or the colour of the face

246

Did you know that –

■ Stanley McCandless (1897-1967) was one of the first teachers to offer a college-level course in Stage Lighting. He was a professor at Yale University from 1925 to 1964 and wrote *Method of Lighting the Stage*, where he proposed the technique of dividing the stage into a grid of areas to illuminate the space

➤ **Lighting for dance**

The emphasis for dance is to illuminate the moving body and less on the face. The addition of side, cross and back lighting is an important element to profile and sculpt the features of the moving body.

Wicked – *Cirencester Creative Dance Academy, Choreographer Katherine Bates, Design and Lighting Design Andy Webb, Photograph © Nik Sheppard*

■ **The lighting areas** for the overhead lighting tend to be based on a regular grid of five areas across by four deep
■ **Flat overhead lighting** with the beams steeply raked at an angle of approximately 80 degrees will provide an overhead wash of precise well-defined downlighting

16 THE LIGHTING PALETTE   A quick start

- **The lighting can be selective**, only seeing the head and shoulders of the actor or the lower body or just the legs of a dancer

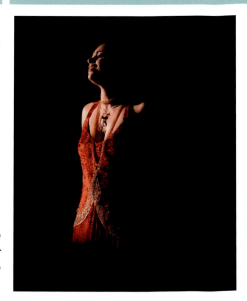

Berlin – *Silo Theatre, Auckland NZ – Lighting Design & Photograph © Andrew Malmo*

'The warm-coloured side lighting from stage right highlights the face and upper body of the actress as she turns into the light.'

❖ *A highlight can draw attention, for example, an actor in partial silhouette back lit by moonlight*

- **Light, shade and shadows** can be very effective; the areas of the stage or set may not need to be equally illuminated

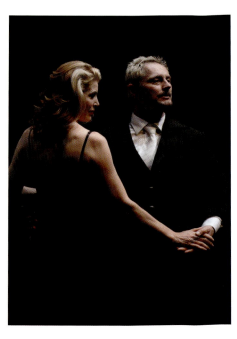

Decadence – *'Potent Pause' productions, Maidment Studio Theatre, Auckland NZ – Lighting Design & Photograph © Andrew Malmo*

'Caught in the moment of time as a single source of cross lighting catches the actor's head and shoulders, highlighting the face and arm of the actress.'

❖ *Walking through shafts of sunlight through a densely wooded area which can be created by using break-up gobos in overhead profile lanterns downlighting the stage. The shadows created obscure what is seen but can add to the visual interest*

❖ *A subtle variation to the intensity of the quality of a front lighting wash can be created by using large break-up gobos but the number of lanterns will need to be increased to ensure adequate illumination*

❖ *Textured light can add realistic visual effects to the setting, for example, gobo break-ups creating shadows projected by sunlight or shafts of light through a window or blind*

■ **Dramatic lighting** or the effects from moving lights may be very impressive but it is important that the action is still illuminated

❖ *The shape and angle of the beam of light can add a dramatic effect like a vertical shaft of light projecting a Les Mis[13] grille gobo on to the stage*

➣ **Motivation – *Where is the light coming from?***

Uncle Vanya – *Birmingham Repertory Theatre production – Lighting Designer Mark Jonathan, Photograph © Robert Day*

'An atmospheric effect as moonlight catches the window frames spilling on to the floor. Low-level side lighting illuminates the actors at either end as if radiating from the lamp in the middle of the table.'

[13] The grille effects as used in the production of *Les Misérables*

For a realistic setting, the aim of the designer is to provide natural lighting and a sense of time and place. The motivation or reason for the illumination may be provided by natural or artificial light sources, sun, moon or daylight, lamp, candle or firelight. This dominant light source provides the direction and influences the way in which the rest of the stage is lit, imitating the natural effect.

❖ *Interior settings may be lit by a natural light source from outside, sun or moonlight, or an artificial source from a light fitting inside*

❖ *Exterior settings are dependent on the effects of natural sources of light, shadows and textures that are created, e.g. sunlight through the trees*

❖ *Non-realistic or abstract styles of productions may require a more stylistic or dramatic form of lighting, e.g. the stark white flat lighting associated with Brechtian epic theatre*

➤ **Composition – *What sort of picture do we want the audience to see?***

We Will Rock You – *Tigz Productions, Sundial Theatre – Lighting Design Andy Webb, Photograph © Nik Sheppard*

A picture can be created by using the lighting to:

■ **Complement** the setting with balanced illumination that reveals everything

■ **Contrast** by using highlights and shadows to focus the audience's attention to a part of the setting or a specific part of the action

■ **Reveal** the action and the setting in proportion to their importance as required

17 USING THE LIGHTING PALETTE   A quick start

➤ Mood – *What do we want the audience to feel about the scene?*

Creating an atmosphere that reflects the mood of the scene is perhaps the main aim of stage lighting. This is achieved by the careful blending of the other three elements of stage lighting: visibility, motivation and composition.

Our House – *Tigz Productions, Bacon Theatre – Lighting Design Andy Webb, Photograph © Nik Sheppard*

17 USING THE LIGHTING PALETTE

A quick start

More info – The tools of lighting

Good lighting should tie together all the visual aspects of the stage with light to paint a picture and create an environment in which the actors can interpret and develop their roles. It should assist them in every way to bring the audience to an understanding of the full meaning and emotion of the unfolding drama.[14]

The tools of lighting

There are four tools that a lighting designer can use to control and blend the elements of stage lighting. The visibility as seen by the eye is affected not only by the reflected brightness but also by the colour, contrast with other illuminated areas, movement of the action and the viewing distance. This all needs to be taken into account.

➤ Intensity

Our House – *Tigz Productions, Bacon Theatre – Lighting Design Andy Webb, Photograph © Nik Sheppard*

The intensity of the light source from the lantern affects the brightness of the reflected light from the object that is being lit. The overall intensity of the lighting can affect the feel of the scene. The intensity and angles of natural light change with the time of day producing different effects.

- ❖ *Afternoon sunlight through a window changing to low sunset can be created by crossfading from higher- to lower-level side lighting lanterns with different colours*
- ❖ *The source of light illuminating the room changes from fading sunlight to an artificial light source being switched on. A downlight source of light is switched on with a practical light fitting, with a change in level of Key and Fill lighting*
- ❖ *Low-level illumination from an overhead hanging artificial light fitting can create an intense feeling of depression with steep angled frontal lighting covering the area illuminated by the practical fitting*

[14] Scene Design and Stage Lighting – Parker & Smith

'The stage lighting designer is more concerned with the brightness of an object than the intensity of its light source. He soon learns that objects of higher brightness generally draw attention on stage. Light attracts! Conversely, darkness conceals.'[15] But this can grab your attention equally and keep the audience on the edge of their seats.

➢ Colour

Our House – *Tigz Productions, Bacon Theatre – Lighting Design Andy Webb,*
Photograph © Nik Sheppard

Colour is a major component used in composing the lighting picture and in creating the mood. It can also be used to enrich the costumes, emphasise the dimension of the setting and enhance the painted decoration of the set. It can set the scene and create the feeling of the icy coldness of a winter day, the coolness of a wet overcast day, the warmth of a spring morning or the heat of a hot summer day.

The effective use of colour is one of the most challenging aspects of stage lighting. Through practice and experience, one develops feel for the use of colour.

❖ *Light tints can be used to soften the lighting subtly*
❖ *Stronger colours can emphasise the more realistic dominant sources of light*
❖ *Deeper colours can provide a contrast*
❖ *The colour of lighting areas can blend together to create an even wash or they can create a contrast*

[15] 'Stage Lighting Design' – Bill Williams

> **Distribution & direction**

War Horse – *National Theatre production – Lighting Design Paule Constable,*
Photograph © Simon Annand

The distribution of the sources of light around the stage, the direction, height and angle of illumination affect the style of the lighting picture that can be created and can add to the mood of the lighting.

❖ *A single source of light will produce a hard shadow like a follow spot. A row of sources of light produce a soft wash of light with hardly any shadows*

❖ *A solo spot pinpoints the action*

❖ *Changing the distribution of the lighting from one area to another moves the focus of attention*

❖ *A steeply raked angle of lighting can produce a dramatic effect. A lower level of light will produce a flatter effect. Shadows change depending upon the direction and angle of the source of the light*

➢ Movement

'The break-up of the beams in the back lighting can be seen as it is picked up in the haze. The slow movement of the rotating gobos added to the magical background of the setting.'

Comedy of Errors – *Cirencester Youth Theatre, Lighting Design Andy Webb, Photograph © Nik Sheppard*

The change in intensity, colour, distribution and direction of the lighting can create movement in the scene. The movement may be a slow and subtle change that the audience may hardly notice but feel emotionally or a fast-moving dynamic effect.

- ❖ *A slow rise in the intensity of light as the level of natural light changes during the day*
- ❖ *The change in the natural colour on a cyc cloth from sunrise to morning light*
- ❖ *A slow crossfade from one area to another or change in colour*
- ❖ *The change in the angle and height in the sources of light as the sun from midday to late afternoon*
- ❖ *A change in direction by cutting from one area to another can produce a dynamic effect*
- ❖ *Colour changes in the lighting areas can be made by using duplicate lanterns, colour scrollers or DMX controlled mixing systems on moving heads or LED fixtures*

267

17 USING THE LIGHTING PALETTE

More info

❖ *Moving heads can provide the unseen flexibility to be repositioned, focused and coloured to light areas during the show or create dynamic moving effects*

❖ *Movement within the beams of light with optical effects, moving projections and rotating gobos*

❖ *Follow spots provide a moving beam of light to follow the main action, focus in on the head and shoulders as used in musical theatre or blend with the general level of lighting to highlight the actor in epic-style drama*

Good facial illumination is important when lighting the show but we have to find ways of combining this with dramatic effects to captivate the audience's imagination and to create that real 'wow' factor of lighting design.

MORE TIPS

■ **Sunlight** – use parallel beams of light from Parcans mounted in the same position to pass through the window in the set to produce a sharp pattern on whatever they strike

■ **Daylight on an overcast day** – a directionless flood of light can be created by a 2.5kW Fresnel with barndoors to produce a soft edged wash

■ **Good lighting** is when the audience doesn't notice it!

More resources – go to

Google 'Stage lighting design'/Bill Williams – Part 1 An introduction to stage lighting – the objectives & qualities of stage lighting

Extras! – Lighting the shows

A lighting designer explains how he has designed the lighting for scenes from two shows.

➢ Lighting for dance – *Swan Lake*

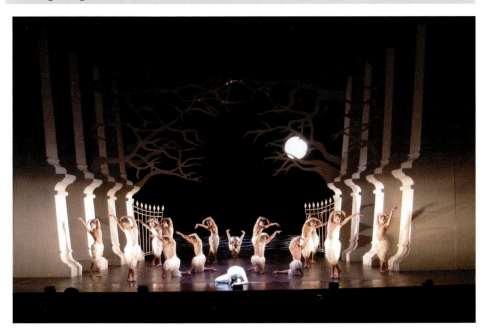

Swan Lake *ballet – Director/Choreographer Mathew Bourne, New Adventures & Backrow Productions – Designer Lez Brotherston, Lighting Design Rick Fisher, Photograph © Mike Rothwell*

'*The swans are almost entirely lit with side light which is arranged on lighting booms in each of the bays between the white columns and a boom that is just in front of the proscenium to cover the forestage.*

　'*The booms in this case have 6 lights on each of them. With a "shin" that is focused across the stage but does not hit the floor and lights the full body of the dancer as long as they are about 2m away from the boom. Then there are similar profiles arranged above this lowest unit to cross light the stage with some of the units focusing up stage to help pick out the facial expressions which are such a part of the production of* Swan Lake.

　'*All lights are kept off the floor which is lit solely with either a wash of backlight parcans or large fresnels (5K and 2K if the stage is especially wide) with scrollers to give as close to a single source colour treatment as possible. This helps the stage to look "cleanly lit". The Prince (downstage centre) is lit with a follow spot.*

　'*The footlights visible in the picture (1K open-faced low profile floods) are used to create illumination and shadows; this particular moment is not one of them.*'

Rick Fisher

17 USING THE LIGHTING PALETTE   Extras!

269

> **Lighting for musical theatre – *Billy Elliot***

Billy Elliot The Musical – *Director Stephen Daldry, Designer Ian MacNeil, Lighting Design Rick Fisher, Photographer Tristram Kenton*

'This brief moment in the finale of Act 1 of Billy Elliot *(Angry Dance) is a particular favourite of mine. As the police land the riot shields on stage the lighting changes instantly to highlight the shields in deep blue from two overhead VL3500Q spots focused tightly to the line of police.*

'The rest of the stage uses almost every other available light in deep red including some boom side lights to light Billy and keep in a drastically different space from the riot police. Haze in the air, which is rarely used in this musical, helps the light to appear sculptural and solid.

'As the dance progresses, the shapes of the spots change with the choreography and the snaps in colour echo the beats of the music and emotion to create isolation of Billy while he is dancing very close to the police.'

Rick Fisher

Lighting jargon – What's it called?

➢ Rigging

Advance bar	Lighting bar hung in front of the proscenium arch
Boom bar	A vertical bar on the side wall of the auditorium or stage used to mount lanterns on boom arms
Lighting bar	Horizontal aluminium bar on which lanterns are hung
Lighting layout plan	A scale drawing of the stage showing the lighting bars and the positions of the lanterns – '**Lighting plot**' (NA)
Lighting rig	A general term for the lanterns hanging on the lighting bars
Patching	Process of temporarily linking or '**hooking up**' (NA) lanterns via outlet sockets to dimmers
1:1 soft patch	Control channel fader No.1 controls dimmer No.1
'T' Bar	Bar attached to a spigot, placed in the top of a stand from which to hang lanterns

➢ Lanterns

Field/beam angle	The spread of the cone of light projected by a lantern measured in degrees
Flagging the lantern	Waving your hand in front of a lantern in the beam of light to see the spread and the extent of the spill light
Floats	Original term for footlights, or small lanterns used on the front of the stage to uplight the face
Footlights	A group of floodlight units mounted in a single row used on the front of the stage – or '**Birdies**' small footlights (NA) also in the (UK)
Fresnel	Adjustable focus lantern, soft edged diffused beam with more spill light than a PC
Front of House (FOH)	In front of the proscenium arch
PC/Prism/Pebble	Adjustable focus lantern, hard/semi-soft edged intense beam with less spill light than a Fresnel
Profile spotlight	Adjustable focus lantern, precise hard edged beam of light that can be soft focused
Throw	Distance from the lantern to the stage

➢ Stage directions

(SL) Stage left	Actor's left when facing the audience
(SR) Stage right	Actor's right when facing the audience
(PS) Prompt side	Traditionally stage left in the UK
(OP) Opposite prompt	Stage right
House left	Left side of the auditorium viewed from the direction of the audience
House right	Right side of auditorium

Up stage	Away from the audience
Down stage	Nearest to the audience
On-stage	Towards the centre of the stage
Off-stage	Away from the centre of the stage towards the wings

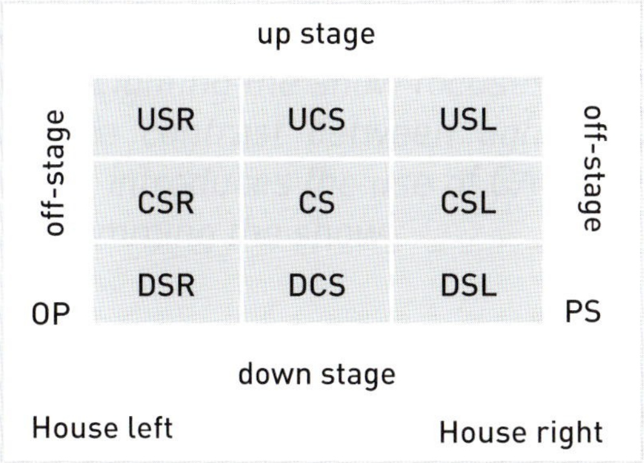

up stage

off-stage	USR	UCS	USL	off-stage
	CSR	CS	CSL	
	DSR	DCS	DSL	

OP   PS

down stage

House left   House right

USL – up stage left, **UCS** – up stage centre, **USR** – up stage right
CSL – centre stage left, **CS** – centre stage, **CSR** – centre stage right
DSL – down stage left, **DCS** – down stage centre, **DSR** – down stage right

➤ The lighting palette

Accent light	Dominant lighting which replicates the main natural source of illumination for the scene
Fill light	Lanterns providing a wash of light adding balance to the Key light
Key light	Lantern providing the main dominant source of illumination or highlight
Open white	'No colour', white light, no colour filter being used
Double colour	'**Doubling up**' (NA), two sheets of the same colour filter mounted in a colour frame to provide a deeper shade of the same colour

LIGHTING JARGON   **What's it called?**

- **Director** – responsible for all the artistic aspects and direction of the production, producing the show on time and within the budget
- **Design team** – artistic team working alongside the director to design and produce the visual look of the production, set, costume, lighting and sound
- **Production Manager** (Technical Director) – used by permanent theatre companies, with similar responsibilities to that of the commercial producers but also responsible for technical preparations and planning

➤ **Lighting Designer LD** – is responsible for the design of the production lighting and effects, and for preparing and producing the drawings and schedules required for the lighting equipment to be installed and connected by the lighting crew. The LD directs the focusing, and supervises the programming/plotting and all artistic elements of the lighting design until the opening of the production.[1]

➤ **Programer** – an experienced lighting desk operator having the knowledge and expertise to assist the Lighting Designer in creating and programming each lighting cue. The role of the programmer has developed with the increased complexity of lighting desks and the use of moving fixtures.

➤ **Chief Electrician** (Production or Head Electrician) is responsible in the professional theatre for organising and supervising the rigging of the lighting equipment by the lighting crew and the running of the production. For small college and amateur productions, this role may also be undertaken by the LD.

➤ **Stage management team**
- **Stage Manager (SM)** – head of the stage management team, responsible for coordinating the production team, the welfare of the actors and the oversight of the rehearsals, supervision of all the technical aspects of mounting the production on-stage and running the show. In North America, the Stage Manager would normally call the show from the lighting and sound control room out front
- **Deputy Stage Manager (DSM)** – responsible for coordinating rehearsals and recording the actors' moves as they are blocked and all the artistic, design and technical decisions that develop during rehearsal in the prompt book. In the UK, the DSM is 'normally on the book', calling the cues for the show from the prompt corner, and when necessary 'giving a line', prompting. In North America, there are no DSMs, only assistant stage managers (ASMs)

Did you know that –

- Traditionally in the UK, the stage has been managed and the show 'run' from the prompt corner which is on the stage left
- In some theatres, the prompt corner and stage manager desk may be on the stage right because of the layout of the building and the position

[1] *Stage Lighting Design*, Bill Williams

of the dressing rooms related to the stage, and it is referred to as a 'bastard prompt' but this is no reflection on the DSM running the corner!
- However, the term Prompt Side is always stage left and Opposite Prompt stage right, no matter the position of the prompt corner
- It is important to retain this convention, as the scenery on touring productions is traditionally marked as PS and OP to show the side of stage that it is to be used or positioned
- The stage manager's desk traditionally has a set of cue lights to all lighting, sound, orchestra, flies, follow spots, etc. that are used to cue the show: red (stand by) and green (go)
- Headsets or 'cans' are now used by the DSM to call the cues, although lights can still be used for a visual reinforcement. The DSM may well be positioned along with lighting and sound in an FOH control position

Preparation before you start to design the lighting

'The designer must know what he is lighting and how he wants the production to look. The designer must be very familiar with the script and all lighting requirements of the production. He must use the qualities of light and objectives of stage lighting to allow him to fully visualize, verbalize and define his design concept and intentions.'[2]

➤ **Read the script**
Prior to meeting with the director, read the script at least twice and record your thoughts.

- First time, try to get the overall feel of the production
- Second time, look for clues that could affect the lighting of each scene, time of day, season, change in mood or emotional flash points
- For musical theatre and dance, listen to and become familiar with the music

➤ **Meet with production team**
This may not always be possible and you may have to just attend the rehearsals, watch, gather your own information and make some creative decisions. However, if you do have the opportunity to meet, talk, listen and discuss with the director and the designers, try to find out:

- How the production is going to be staged and the basic lighting requirements
- The lighting requirements of the set design
- What colours will be used in the set and costumes
- The style of lighting required, natural, realistic, abstract, lighting for dance
- The feel of the production reflecting the emotional qualities developed by the playwright or the director's and designer's interpretation of the script

[2] *Stage Lighting Design*, Bill Williams

18 PREPARING TO LIGHT THE SHOW

A quick start

- The changes in mood or atmosphere, season or time of day that need to be created
- How the lighting will be used to select areas and to create special effects
- The positions of the main acting areas, 'specials', solo areas and any special effects
- Budget available for the hire of additional equipment and purchase of colour filters, gobos, etc.
- Production timetable, time available for rigging, focusing, plotting, tech run and dress rehearsals

➤ **Research**
  - **Set design** – study the model of the set, identify any obvious source of illuminating windows or light fittings, photograph the model and scene changes, obtain a copy of the plan and elevation
  - **Costume designs** – study the sketches for the designs, photograph the designs and endeavour to obtain samples of the main coloured materials to be used
  - **Visit the theatre space** – walk the stage, view all the rigging positions, estimate the lengths of throw and the angle of illumination of the lanterns, check out the local electrics staff available for the production. Obtain a copy of the stage plan and elevation showing the layout of the lighting bars and the permanently installed circuit outlet socket numbers or make a survey drawing to produce your own plans
  - **Check the equipment available:**
    Lanterns – the numbers of each type, make and model
    Dimmer packs/racks – the total number of dimmers mains electrical power available
    Control desk – make and model, specification control circuits, memory facilities, moving fixtures
  - **Attend rehearsals** – note the positions of the main acting areas, entrances and movement of the actors, as this can suggest the direction of the lighting; check the blocking with the DSM
  - **Play around with your ideas** – try to visualise the lighting of the action and the set, the angles of the lighting, the colours that might be used and the changes in the states of lighting
  - **Record your ideas** – sketch out visual ideas and plans, experiment, talk and share ideas with the director and designers

'Creative lighting is the technique of reproducing the characteristics of natural lighting in order to stimulate specific subconscious feelings.'

> **Online video link – 18.1 Designing the show**
> https://vimeo.com/123718051

GLOBAL JARGON
- **Chief Electrician** (UK) – **Production/Head/Master Electrician** (NA)

A quick start

18 PREPARING TO LIGHT THE SHOW

More info – Preparing a plan

It is important to have a lighting layout plan of the venue that you are working in to fully understand the layout of the lighting system and to use it efficiently. The plan is like a 'Road Map' that will guide you to success and without it you may get lost.

Lighting layout plan

A layout plan of the stage and auditorium should show the positions of lighting bars and the layout of all the outlet sockets and circuit numbers. The plan is used to record the position of the lanterns and the dimmer circuit numbers that control them.

➤ **Making a survey and plan of the lighting system**

If a plan is not available when working in a new venue, the first thing to do is to make a survey plan, even if it is only a quick sketch. The basic measurements of the space will also be required.

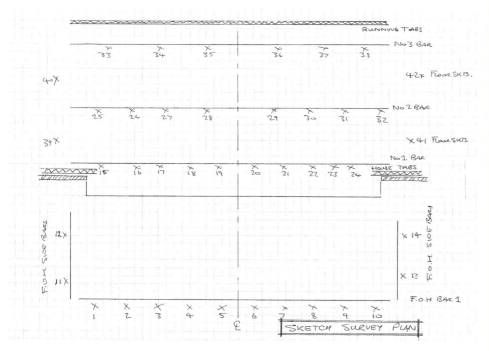

Sketch survey plan – GMSL

■ Draw up a sketch survey plan with the positions of all the lighting bars. If possible, use squared paper – it will help you keep the drawing in proportion. Find out where all the circuit outlet sockets are and mark their positions using a cross and record the socket numbers

- If the sockets are not numbered, work out a sequence starting from stage right to left on each lighting bar, and from front of house to the up stage bars
- Number all the sockets, so that they can be clearly seen from the stage, as this will help with rigging and the identification of the lanterns
- Draw up a scaled plan using a CAD program or
- Make an accurate scaled drawing of the lighting layout plan on a sheet of A3 or A4 squared paper, depending upon the size required, using the information from the sketch survey drawing. Use a centre line as marked on the example plan to help keep the layout and the positions of the bars and sockets symmetrical
- Use a stencil to draw small circles to mark the positions of the outlet sockets and place the circuit number inside the circle
- Keep the original copy safe and use it as the master for photocopying. A3-size plans are used for designing the layout of lanterns. Reducing the size on a photocopier to A4 will provide a useful size to carry round with you to quickly identify the circuit outlet socket numbers

➤ **Scaled plans**

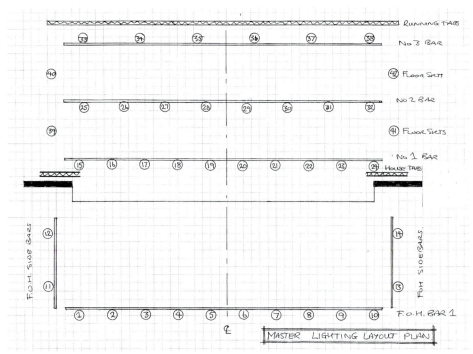

Lighting layout plan scaled drawing – GMSL

Using a scaled drawing of the plan gives a better idea of the usage of space and the positioning of the lanterns and it is essential to use when working on a medium- to large-size stage

- A measured survey will be needed to draw up an accurate scaled plan
- The lantern stencils are produced to fit either a 1:25 or 1:50 metric scale
- The most common scale used in the theatre is 1:25 or ½" to 1ft in the American system or what is sometimes called the 'English units'. Theatre designers also use this scale for their drawings and models in order to provide sufficient detail
- 1:50m or ¼":1ft scales are used for very large venues where it would be impossible to fit the drawing on to a large enough sheet
- 1:25 is a standard metric scale used for theatre drawings that is:

1mm Drawing size		Represents 25mm Actual (full) size	
1mm	=	25mm	(.025m)
4mm	=	100mm	(.100m)
10mm	=	250mm	(.250m)
20mm	=	500mm	(.500m)
40mm	=	1000mm	(1.000m)
80mm	=	2000mm	(2.000m)
160mm	=	4000mm	(4.000m)
500mm	=	5000mm	(5.000m)

- On a 1:25 metric scale drawing, 1mm represents 25mm full-size measurement. The use of a scaled rule removes the need to calculate the scaled measurement as the graduations are marked with the full-size measurement
- Start with a centre line and construct the position of the proscenium arch, front of stage, side and rear walls. Draw in the positions of the lighting bars
- When working on a scale drawing, it is possible to plan the accurate positions and the spacing of the lanterns on the bars, which can then be replicated by Lx crew when rigging on-stage

18 PREPARING TO LIGHT THE SHOW

More info

Extras! – Working with CAD (computer aided design)

Lighting layout plans and elevations can be constructed by using a computer drawing program, 2D plan drawing software or a dedicated stage lighting Computer Aided Design (CAD) program.

Computer software

➤ **Draw/ 2D CAD programs**
Drawings can be produced by using the CIE basic lantern symbols which can be easily constructed.

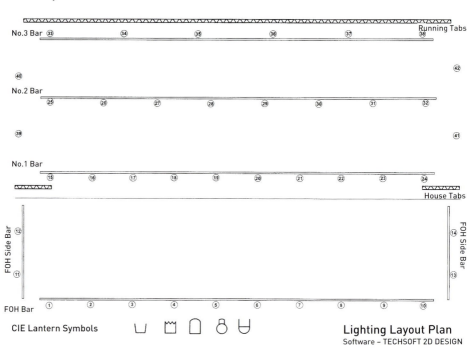

CAD plan – GMSL

- Draw programs can be found on most standard computer software and they can be used to produce a schematic lighting plan. A4-size printouts can be enlarged to A3 on a photocopier to provide a larger working plan. The major drawback is that these drawings will not be to scale which makes it little more than a sketch but it can be used for a small production
- 2D CAD programs can be used to construct the basic CIE lighting symbols and lighting layout plans plans or 'plots' to scale

CAD Programs used for stage lighting

There are many CAD Computer Aided Drafting programs used by lighting designers to create rig plans of their designs.

These can be generic CAD programs such as AutoCAD or programs specifically designed for use by Lighting Designers and Technicians. The majority of lantern manufacturers now have CAD symbols of their products downloadable from their website. Many of these are however complex 3D Models that may require some work to be usable. Other sites such as Modelbox (www.modelbox.co.uk) also have 2D lantern symbols free to use.

All of these programs will be able to do some or all of the following:

- Draw 2D Plans and Sections of the stage and scenery with lantern symbols and information
- Generate paperwork directly from the plan to produce equipment lists of lanterns and accessories, details of channel and dimmer allocations, colour calls and power requirements
- Create 3D Views
- Create Photo realistic images of lighting states
- Pre-visualise the show allowing prerecording of lighting cues, looks and groups

Stage lighting software

The following software is commercially available and has been specifically designed for the theatre and entertainment lighting designers.

➤ **LxDesigner** – suitable for FE college use and possibly small venues

LxDesigner is an easy-to-use design environment for stage lighting, suitable for use in schools, colleges and small venues. 'Included are a number of libraries which contain symbols for the various set, rigging and fixtures used in the design process. The plan is built up by simply dragging and dropping the required symbols on to the drawing area or by using one of the built-in tools such as the truss builder. The package has a number of built-in reports which can be used to generate the paperwork associated with the design such as gel, rigging and equipment calls.' There are additional add-on features available, providing side, front and perspective views. The website provides a comprehensive set of demo movies providing online training tutorials that click automatically through the stages of its use.[3]

➤ **Vectorworks Spotlight**

Seen by many as the standard for theatre lighting designers and available on Mac and Windows PC, Spotlight is the dedicated entertainment lighting version of this popular 2D/3D drafting package. Spotlight is supplied with libraries of lanterns from all the major manufacturers allowing drag and drop design from the Resource Browser. Also included are libraries of Truss, set pieces and drapes.

[3] www.lxdesign.co.uk; www.kave.co.uk – Kave Theatre Services information on LxDesigner

19 Planning the design

A quick start – Lantern layout plan

Using stencils to plan a lantern layout plan on paper

More info – Which lantern to use & where

Selecting lanterns, wattage, length of throw, narrow and wide-angle lanterns

Extras! – Beam spread/field angles

Understanding the data, comparing field angles, calculating the beam spread

A quick start – Lantern layout plan

'Planning on paper gives me the space to play around creatively and form my ideas. I like to start by working on a large 1:25 scale A1 size plan of the stage and set on a drawing board as it helps me to visualise the space and the position of the sources of light. As I draw in the positions of the lanterns with a stencil I plan the spacing on the lighting bar as it is in "real time". When the creative thinking is complete then I transfer my plan to the computer to do all the detailed planning and paper work.' Andy Webb, Lighting designer

Constructing a lantern layout plan

Some designers find it easier to start to visualise their ideas and plan their design on paper, while others will start using a CAD program.

When working on a scaled plan drawing, it is essential to use lantern stencils to plan the positions of the lanterns. The CIE international symbol stencils are fairly satisfactory for small-size rigs. For larger rigs, the 1:25 scaled manufacturer's symbol stencils should be used in order to make sure that there is enough space to fit all the lanterns on to the lighting bars.

➤ **Guidelines when drawing a plan**
- Draw the lantern in the position and angled in the direction that it is going to be used

- **Field/beam angle**, e.g. 24/44° are frequently used to identify the type of Profile spot
  Acclaim 24/44° zoomspot – short throw distance
  Acclaim 18/34° zoomspot – medium throw distance
  Acclaim Axial 18/34° zoomspot – long throw distance
  Pacific 12/28° – long throw distance

- **North America** lanterns are identified by the lens diameter and the focal length
  Altman Ellipsoidal 360Q 6 x 12 – 6 inch dia. lens x 12 inch focal length but this doesn't give any information on the beam angle or spread

NB: each manufacturer produces their own range of lanterns with their own model names. See Lighting resources page 000 ("Makes & models of lanterns – a quick guide)

Field/beam angle

The size of the cone of light projected by a lantern increases with the distance and length of throw.

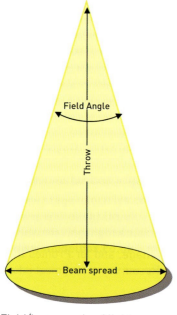

Field/beam angle of light

➤ **The field/beam angle** quoted in degrees by a manufacturer indicates the size of the beam, e.g. 18° a narrow beam, 34° a wide beam. The minimum/maximum angles quoted by the manufacturers for each model indicate the characteristics and performance of the lantern and how and where they can be used. The diameter of the cone of light projected by a lantern can be calculated by making a scaled drawing of the length of throw from the lantern and the field/beam angle.

➤ **The length of throw from a lantern**
It is necessary to calculate the true length of throw by constructing a right-angle triangle using the vertical height of the lantern to the stage and the horizontal distance to the centre of the lighting area. This can be measured on-stage or found from the lantern layout plan and side elevation drawing of the lighting rig. The triangle can be constructed as a scaled drawing on 5mm square grid paper using a 1:50 scale where 4 squares represent 1m as below. The third side represents the true length of throw that can be measured with a scale rule or calculated from the grid by rotating the length of the side with a compass into the vertical position.

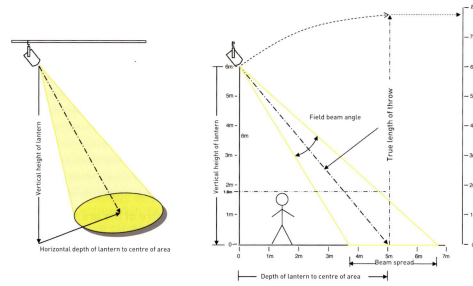

Constructing the true length of throw of a beam of light

➤ **The true length of throw from a lantern can be found on the following chart:**

		True length of throw (metres) – lantern to centre of the area						
Vertical height of lantern	**10m**	10.40	10.70	11.20	11.60	12.20	12.80	13.40
	9m	9.50	9.80	10.30	10.80	11.40	12.00	12.70
	8m	8.50	8.90	9.40	10.00	10.60	11.30	12.00
	7m	7.60	8.10	8.60	9.20	9.90	10.60	11.40
	6m	6.70	7.20	7.80	8.50	9.20	10.00	
	5m	5.80	6.40	7.10	7.80	8.60		
	4m	5.00	5.65	6.40	7.20			
		3m	**4m**	**5m**	**6m**	**7m**	**8m**	**9m**
		Horizontal depth from lanterns to centre of the area						

➤ **The spread of a beam of light**
The spread or the diameter of a beam of light can be found on the following chart by relating the true length of throw from the lantern to the centre of the area and the field/beam angle.

Extras! – Beam spread/field angles

When planning your lighting, it is useful to know the basic characteristics of each lantern, its potential throw, the size of the beam spread over a set distance and how bright the pool of light will be.

Understanding the data

Manufacturers' catalogues provide the specifications for their range of generic lanterns specifying the size of lens, beam spread and light output. This may be different for a similar lantern from another manufacturer. Following are some examples from one manufacturer:

➤ **Selecon – Fresnel & PC lantern data:**

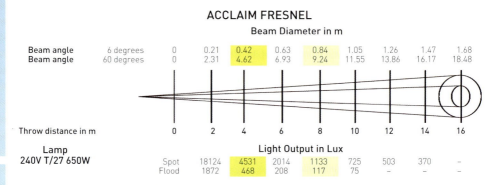

ACCLAIM FRESNEL
Beam Diameter in m

| Beam angle | 6 degrees | 0 | 0.21 | 0.42 | 0.63 | 0.84 | 1.05 | 1.26 | 1.47 | 1.68 |
| Beam angle | 60 degrees | 0 | 2.31 | 4.62 | 6.93 | 9.24 | 11.55 | 13.86 | 16.17 | 18.48 |

Throw distance in m: 0, 2, 4, 6, 8, 10, 12, 14, 16

Light Output in Lux

Lamp 240V T/27 650W								
Spot	18124	4531	2014	1133	725	503	370	–
Flood	1872	468	208	117	75	–	–	–

Fresnel beam angle – Philips Selecon

- ■ **Beam diameter** measured in metres
- ■ **Length of throw** measured in metres
- ■ **Light output** measured in Lux
- ■ **The optimum length of throw** should have a light output of around 2000 Lux

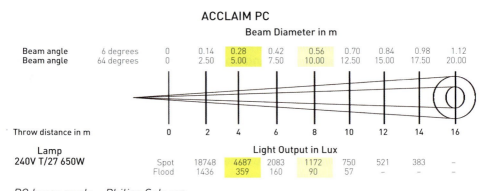

ACCLAIM PC
Beam Diameter in m

| Beam angle | 6 degrees | 0 | 0.14 | 0.28 | 0.42 | 0.56 | 0.70 | 0.84 | 0.98 | 1.12 |
| Beam angle | 64 degrees | 0 | 2.50 | 5.00 | 7.50 | 10.00 | 12.50 | 15.00 | 17.50 | 20.00 |

Throw distance in m: 0, 2, 4, 6, 8, 10, 12, 14, 16

Light Output in Lux

Lamp 240V T/27 650W								
Spot	18748	4687	2083	1172	750	521	383	–
Flood	1436	359	160	90	57	–	–	–

PC beam angle – Philips Selecon

Extras!

19 PLANNING THE DESIGN

The beam diameter and light output vary depending upon the:

- **Length of throw** of the beam
- **Size of the beam** spot to Flood focus
- **Optimum length of throw – 6m**

➤ Comparing Fresnel & PC lantern data

	Field/beam angle	Throw	Beam dia	Light output
Fresnel	Spot focus – 6 degrees	6m	0.63m	2014 Lux
PC	Spot focus – 4 degrees	6m	0.42m	2083 Lux
Fresnel	Flood focus – 60 degrees	4m	4.62m	458 Lux
PC	Flood focus – 64 degrees	4m	5.00m	359 Lux

Spot focus at a 6m throw
- **Fresnel** has a slightly wider beam but a lower light output
- **PC** has a narrower beam and a slight increase in the light output

Flood focus at a 6m throw
- Compare the beam sizes and light outputs for the Flood focus

➤ Selecon – Axial zoomspot lantern data:

ACCLAIM AXIAL ZOOMSPOTS 18°–34° & 24°–44°

Beam Diameter in m

Beam angle	18 degrees	0	0.63	1.27	1.90	2.53	3.17	3.80	4.43	5.07
Beam angle	34 degrees	0	1.22	2.45	3.67	4.89	6.11	7.34	8.56	9.78
Beam angle	24 degrees	0	0.85	1.70	2.55	3.40	4.25	5.10	5.95	6.80
Beam angle	44 degrees	0	1.62	3.23	4.85	6.46	8.08	9.70	11.31	12.93

| Throw distance in m | 0 | 2 | 4 | 6 | 8 | 10 | 12 | 14 | 16 |

Light Output in Lux

Lamp 240V T/27 650W									
18°	Peak	27124	6781	3014	1695	1085	753	554	424
34°	Peak	16252	4063	1806	1016	650	451	332	254
24°	Peak	23752	5938	2639	1485	950	660	485	371
44°	Peak	12500	3125	1389	781	500	347	255	195

Acclaim Axial beam angle – Philips Selecon

The beam diameter and light output vary depending upon the:

- **Lantern beam angle** – 18/34 or 24/44
- **Length of throw** of the beam
- **Diameter of the beam** – spot or Flood focus

➤ **Preproduction preparation**
- **Equipment list/instrument schedule**
  Showing the position and type of lantern, colour filter, circuit outlet socket number, dimmer and channel control number

Hanging position	Lantern no. plan L–R	Lantern	Colour filter no.	Circuit socket no.	Dimmer no.	Desk control channel no.
				Hard patching/Hook up		
Lx 1.	1	Fresnel	L152	1	1	C1
Lx 1.	2	PC	L152	3	4	C4
Lx 1.	3	PC	L136	5	3	C3
Lx 1.	4	PC	L136	6	3	C3
Lx 1.	5	Profile	L152	7	6	C6
Lx 1.	6	PC	L154	9	2	C2
Lx 1.	7	Fresnel	L154	10	5	C5
Lx 1.	8	Profile	L154	11	6	C6
Lx 2.	9	Fresnel	L152	12	7	C7
Lx 2.	10	Fresnel	L152	13	8	C8

- **Patching/hook-up** – the lanterns are connected via the outlet circuits that are hard patched to the dimmer packs so that the lighting desk control channel numbers match the lighting areas
- **Basic hard patch plan** – showing the layout of the numbered dimmer units and sockets on the dimmer pack, e.g. the plug top of the outlet circuit No.1 is patched to dimmer No.1, control by channel No.1

Dimmer pack No.1

Dimmer No Channel No	Dimmer 1/C1	Dimmer 2/C2	Dimmer 3/C3	Dimmer 4/C4	Dimmer 5/C5	Dimmer 6/C6
Socket	1	9	5	3	10	7
Socket			6			

Dimmer pack No.2

Dimmer 1/C7	Dimmer 2/C8	Dimmer 3/C9	Dimmer 4/C10	Dimmer 5/C11	Dimmer 6/C12
12	13	16	Flood	Flood	
14	15	17			

QUICK TIPS

■ **Planning a lighting rig** – lay out the lanterns on the stage under the bars in the position they will be hung to light the areas; stand back and check your layout and make any adjustments; record on to a plan

■ Lighting small shows provides practical experience and helps to develop a greater understanding of the effects produced by individual lanterns, the size and quality of the beam of light and the length of throw

■ The experience gained will assist you to be able to visualise effects of the lighting when planning on paper and creating a lighting design

20 THE DESIGN PROCESS

A quick start

- **Hire/shop list** – list of equipment and accessories to be hired in
- **Risk assessment** – produce a risk assessment for all aspects of the lighting installation
- **Magic sheet**[6] – make a lighting area crib sheet/plan, a simplified diagrammatic plan showing the direction, colour and control channel numbers of the lanterns lighting each of the main areas on an A4 sheet of paper

➤ **Preproduction paperwork**

There are various lists that can be generated from CAD lighting software direct from the lighting plan. Also there is other stand-alone software that will create all the paperwork from an initial input of data, see 'More resources – Lightwrite 5'.

➤ **Check your designs**

- **Talk** to the director and designer about your designs
- **Check** the colours selected on the colours of the set and costumes
- **Attend** rehearsals to check there are no major changes to the blocking of the actors' moves that may affect the lighting areas
- **Confirm** with the director the sequence of lighting changes and the intended feel to each state of the lighting
- **Produce** a cue outline sheet, a numbered list of all the changes in the states of lighting, discuss or circulate to the director and DSM; expect some feedback and modifications
- **Attend** the final run-through rehearsals; check the cue synopsis and familiarise the actors' positions and moves related to the intended lighting of the acting areas

➤ **Communicate your designs**

- **Confirm hire list** and expenditure with the producer/production manager and place order
- **Confirm cue list** with DSM who will be running the show
- **Provide copies** of the lantern layout plans, equipment, patching, lighting bar lists, colour and cable call to the chief electrician and Lx crew
- **Meet** with the chief electrician and/or crew to talk about your intentions for the lighting design and to discuss any problems over the rig

---

[6] 'Magic list' name credited to Tom Skelton circa 1970 – Bill Williams; a similar process is also described by Francis Reid in *Lighting the Amateur Stage*

GLOBAL JARGON

- **Open white (OW)** (UK) – **'no color'** (NA) **NC** or **N/C** standard abbreviation used when marking up a plan
- **Equipment list** (UK) – **Instrument schedule** (NA)
- **Rigging to hang the lanterns** (UK) – **The Hang** (NA)
- **Lantern layout plan** (UK) – **The lighting plot** (NA)
- **Hard patching of lanterns to dimmers** (UK) – **Hook-up** (NA)
- **Hire list** (UK) – **Shop order** (NA)
- **Hire** (UK) – **Rental** (NA)

MORE TIPS

- An hour spent planning and preparing is worth two wasted on-stage!
- Use a mini Mag-lite torch with a colour swatch to try out the effects of the colour filters on the set model, samples of costume materials and the back of your hand for flesh tones

More resources – go to

www.mckernon.com – Lightwrite 5 is a unique cross between a spreadsheet and a database, designed specifically to manage professional lighting design paperwork.

'Lightwrite understands what designers and electricians do with their paperwork. It knows that dimmers and circuits shouldn't be overloaded, that striplights have more than one color, it organizes your worknotes, and provides tools to design color scrolls and specify moving light wheels. It can find mistakes, reconcile two sets of paperwork, figure circuit and dimmer needs, renumber or rearrange channels and dimmers, and assign dimmers automatically.'[7]

Points for action

Quickies!

- Log on to www.mckernon.com: click on to a short video tour

[7] www.mckernon.com – product information

✓ **Fly out the bar** – with a sash cord measuring twice the required height over the bar to set the Trim/Dead height of the bar as the side elevation drawing

✓ **Fly out the loom** of singles or multicore cables

➤ **Hard patching** – power distribution
The distribution of the power via dimmer circuits to lanterns and via circuit breakers to DMX fixtures.

- **Hard patch up the loom** to the localised house patching panels or 'Waylines' as planned on the Lx bar equipment list

➤ **Soft patching** – use the control desk software to:
- **Assign the control channels** on the lighting desk to the DMX 512 addresses of the dimmers, fixtures and effects as planned on the patching/hooking-up schedule

The focus – a large show

When focusing on-stage lighting, designers use a combination of hand actions and phrases to direct the operators.

The method of focusing was covered in detail in Chapter 3 'Working with lanterns – A quick start' and Chapter 15 'Other angles of lighting – Extras!'.

Each LD may use their own variations so you should be ready to adapt to their style. The following will give you some starting points:

➤ **Actions when focusing**
- **Standing on-stage with back facing the focuser** – spot focus the beam and centre it on to the back of the head and shoulders – lock off the adjustments
- **Arms raised moving hands outwards** – enlarge the beam until the hands stop moving
- **Arms raised moving hands inwards** – reduce the beam size
- **Arms raised hands stop** – lock off the zoom focus on the lantern
- **Single arm raised hand moving in** – Profile/Axial: cut the beam in using the shutter on the opposite side of the lantern; Fresnel/PC: cut the barndoor in on the same side of the lantern

➤ **Focusing jargon**
- **'Can I see number 6'** – raise channel 6 to 90%
- **'Hit my shoulders'** – spot focus the beam and centre it on the back of the shoulders
- **'Beam at my heels'** – focus the beam to start from the heels, used by dance LDs to direct side lighting
- **'Open it up', 'Close it down'** – enlarge and reduce the size of the beam
- **'Flag that'** or **'Flaggit'** – wave your hand in the beam of light to indicate the cover
- **'Move it on-stage'** or **'Move it off-stage'** – move the beam towards the centre stage and away from the centre

- **'Lock it off'** or **'Lock that'** – tighten the adjusting nut or wing nut on the lantern suspension and tilt so that it doesn't move
- **'Shutter in the top'** – Profile/Ellipsoidal: move the bottom shutter in
- **'Shutter in the bottom'** – Profile/Ellipsoidal: move the top shutter in
- **'Sharpen it'** or **'Soften it'** – harden and soften the focus
- **'Top door in'** – Fresnel/PC: move the top barndoor down
- **'Hold it'** – stop moving the shutter or barndoor
- **'Ghost it'** – take the level of light down to 25%
- **'Next'** – moving on to focus the next lantern on the bar

➤ **Focusing moving fixtures**

Moving fixtures are focused in a similar way to generic lanterns: tilt and pan followed by adjustments to the beam size, colour and pattern. The main difference is that the change is produced on the lighting desk by moving the control wheels assigned to the fixture personality. The new position, beam size, colour and pattern will be programmed as a 'follow on' cue in preparation for the next cue.

- Moving fixtures can take a long time to focus so it is a good idea to pre-program a number of preset focused positions that can be stored in the memory as named palette or focus group
- It is important to store them with meaningful names that can easily be identified with the limited number of characters that can be used on the small lighting desk screen if a monitor is not being used
- If it is necessary during the rehearsals to readjust the position or any other attributes of a preset focused position, the other cues where the palette has been used will automatically be updated

Automated lighting rigs

Theatre companies running a season of productions are moving towards using automated lighting rigs to accommodate the requirements of lighting the repertoire.

At the Royal Shakespeare Theatre the overhead area lighting is provided by an automated lighting rig that is suspended from the computer controlled powered flying winches over the large thrust stage.

The moving heads fixtures are mounted in 30 clusters that are suspended from a series of tracks that can be moved into 53 different positions over the large thrust stage and surrounding auditorium. Each cluster has two moving heads suspended from a pallet that can be independently moved up and down to adjust the angle of lighting. They can also lowered to stage or parked at the level of the technical gallery for rigging and maintenance. The movement created on the cluster by panning and tilting of the moving head or lowering or raising pallet during the show is stabilized by the use of a system called 'Lightlock'. This has been specifically designed and developed by the RSC lighting department to remove the pendulum effect.[11] (See chapter 15 Other Angles of illumination – More info)

[11] 'Thrusting, Flexible and Green – Royal Shakespeare Theatre' A K Bennett-Hunter, ABTT 'Sightline' Journal of Theatre Technology and Design

21 THE LIGHTING PROCESS   Extras!

'Allo 'Allo – A rural French café, midday with the bright sunlight coming in through the stage right door – Skip Mort

'Allo 'Allo – evening, the main focus of the lighting is on the action in the centre – Skip Mort

'Allo 'Allo – *The pantry inset scene; the acting area was larger than the scenery backing – Skip Mort*

'Allo 'Allo – *The scenery backings to the doors need to be lit – Skip Mort*

Did you know that –

■ Tracking cue method was originally used by manual dimmer operators who were only concerned with changes in dimmer levels

■ **'Full up to Finish'** was a term used in musical and variety theatre before modern stage spotlighting. To increase the dramatic effect for a solo or duet the singers would be picked up by two follow spots or 'Limes' with the general stage lighting from the overhead battens being reduced to provide rich wash of colour. At the final crescendo of the song the overhead lighting would be brought up 'full up to finish' creating a dramatic effect to instant applause.[16]

Lighting the show at the Royal Shakespeare Theatre

Programming at the RST – Photo by Matt Peel RSC

The illustration shows lighting programmer and designer are working together lighting a large show at the RST. The lighting programmer on the left is programming a 'grandMA' lighting desk. The lighting designer is on the right with his cue list on the laptop; detailed lighting plans on the desk and a 'Magic Sheet' on the monitor in front showing a diagrammatic layout of the lighting plan for quick reference.

The lighting designer creates the picture of light for each cue by directing the overhead moving fixtures, position, movement, colour and gobo pattern. The required angle of wash light from the layers of generic lanterns is selected along with the scroller colour and the level of light. The programmer programs the desk to create the desired lighting as directed by the LD, building up the states of lighting and recording/saving the cues.

"With the increased use of automated fixtures in the rig as at the RSC, lighting design is becoming more and more a response to the situation and the action rather than trying to pre-visualise the lighting pictures to be created as with a generic rig" – Rick Fisher, 'Merchant of Venice' RST

[16] David Edmund – Stage Manager, Theatre Royal Exeter

Lighting from the show – *Our House*

Our House – *Tigz Productions, Bacon Theatre – Lighting Design Andy Webb, Photographer Nik Sheppard*

'The umbrella dance sequence, note the gobo patterned back lighting' – © Nik Sheppard

'The rain effect projected from the front with the strong blue back lighting from the moving heads and light blue side lighting.' – © Nik Sheppard

'The prison visiting scene: strong down lighting with precise follow spots lighting the faces of the two down stage actors, cutting in at an acute angle from either side.'
– © Nik Sheppard

'The car sequences with moving projected background and the three actors in the front illuminated by steeply raked cross lighting to avoid spill light falling onto the screen.'
– © Nik Sheppard

'The dance sequence: note the lead actor's face being lit by two tightly focused follow spots cutting in at an acute angle from either side FOH and not from the standard rear of the auditorium positions.' – © Nik Sheppard

EXTRA TIPS

- When focusing moving fixtures, move the 'tilt' first followed by the 'pan' to prevent the head from 'flipping' over to get from one position to another
- Know your lighting desk and how it works before you start to program the show
- The specialist role of a programmer is starting to be seen as that of an assistant to the lighting designer also as a pathway to becoming an LD. Hence the emphasis put on programming training in technician courses in Theatre and Drama Schools.

Points for action

Takes longer

- If you have access to a colour scroller, try setting it up and programming some colour changes

A proper job!

- Explore your lighting desk to find out the programming protocol
- If you have access to a moving head fixture, try setting it up and programming a simple set of positions for the beam

Lighting jargon – What's it called?

➤ Abbreviations & stage terms

ALD	Association of Lighting Designers
ASM	Assistant stage manager
Blocking	Recording the actors' moves and entrances related to the text
Cyclorama/Cyc	White rear wall or backcloth used to mix coloured light and create sky effects
DSM	Deputy stage manager (UK), attends all rehearsals, keeps the 'book' and runs the show
L. D.	**Lighting Designer** (UK) – **Lighting Director** (NA)
SM	Stage manager
Stage director (NA)	Performs the same role as the DSM in the UK
The 'book'	The master copy of the script which contains blocking, lists of furniture and props, cues for the show
'Walker'	An ASM who walks the stage when setting and plotting to check the level of illumination

➤ The lighting control desk

Chase	Continuous repeated sequence of flashing lights produced by the effects function on a lighting control desk as used on neon signs
Dipless crossfade	Channel levels set at the same level on both presets remain at the same intensity
Flashing through	Raising each control channel in succession to check that the lantern or fixture is working after rigging and before each performance – '**Stepping through**' (NA)
Light board	Alternative term for lighting control desk
Master fader	Having the overriding control of a group of channel faders
'On the board'	Lighting operator referring back to when the lighting was controlled by a switchboard and resistance dimmers
Preset lighting	Lighting an open set prior to the audience entering the auditorium
Scene preset	Group of individual channel faders on a lighting control desk that control the dimmers
Soft patching	Electronic patching a DMX address to a control channel on the lighting desk
'Tab warmers'	Lanterns focused to light the front curtain 'tabs', often with a warm colour

➤ Lanterns

Cyc – asymmetrical	Fixed focus Flood, soft edged even wash directed downwards by an asymmetrical reflector
Generic lanterns	Non-automated lanterns, often referred to as Generics
PC/Prism/Pebble	Adjustable focus lantern, hard/semi-soft edged intense beam with less spill light than a Fresnel
Profile spotlight	Adjustable focus lantern, precise hard edged beam of light that can be soft focused
Flood – symmetrical	Fixed focus lantern, soft edged even wash having a symmetrical reflector
Fresnel	Adjustable focus lantern, soft edged diffused beam with more spill light than a PC
Parcan	Fixed focus lantern, intense near parallel oval beam of light that can be rotated

➤ Rigging on-stage

Dips	Floor circuits/sockets mounted under the stage floor to connect practical fittings or side lighting
Dip traps	Metal flaps mounted in the stage floor providing access to floor sockets
Fit-up	Assembling the scenery on stage and rigging the lanterns
Hard patching	Process of temporarily linking or 'hooking up' lanterns via outlet sockets to the dimmers
The in	Shortened term for '**Get-in**' moving the set and lighting into the theatre – '**Load-in**' (NA) – **Pack-in**' (SH)
I.W.B.	Internally Wired Barrel, having outlet sockets mounted on the bar internally wired to an end box – '**Connector strips**' (NA)
Jumper	A short extension cable not a woolly jumper! – '**Extension cord**' (NA) or in motion picture production '**Stinger**'
Ladders	Suspended framework in the wings to hang lanterns from for side lighting
Lighting rig	General term for the lanterns hanging on the lighting bars
Loom	A group of cables tied together as from a lighting bar – '**Hod**' (NA)
The out	Shortened term for 'Get-out' moving the set and lighting into the theatre – '**Load-out**' (NA) – '**Pack-out**' (SH)
Patch panel	Hardwired circuits terminated with flexible cables and numbered plug tops passing through a holed comb panel mounted below the dimmer units
Practical	A light fitting, e.g. a desk light, which may be switched on by the actor
Rigging	Term used for hanging lanterns and equipment
TRS	Extension cables are made up from tough rubber shield cable, which is used as an abbreviated name

345

Part three: Lighting resources

- ⟩ Online video resources

- Technical info.

- Websites

- Key notes!

Credits

Bibliography

› Online video resources

Part 1 – Lighting Technician

Lanterns, Dimmers & Control

1.1   **Understanding the lighting system**
https://vimeo.com/123717415

2.1   **Five types of lanterns**
https://vimeo.com/123717416

3.1   **Adjusting lanterns**
https://vimeo.com/123717417

4.1   **Dimmers**
https://vimeo.com/123717418

4.2   **Dimmers, patch panels & power supplies**
https://vimeo.com/123717419

5.1   **Manual control desks**
https://vimeo.com/123717494

5.2   **Memory control desks**
https://vimeo.com/123717495

7.1   **Safety when working at heights**
https://vimeo.com/123717496

Colour, Gobos & Effects

9.1   **Using gobos**
https://vimeo.com/123717500

10.1   **Moving effects and fixtures**
https://vimeo.com/123717501

11.1   **Gobo slide projection**
https://vimeo.com/123717626

12.1   **Special effects**
https://vimeo.com/123717627

13.1   **Strobe and black lighting**
https://vimeo.com/123717628

13.2   **Flashes and bangs**
https://vimeo.com/123717628

FAST FORWARD

Online Video Resources

> ## Online video resources

Part 2 – Lighting Designer

Lighting the Performance Space

14.1 Angles of illumination
https://vimeo.com/123717962

14.2 Three angles of lighting
https://vimeo.com/123717963

14.3 Flat area lighting
https://vimeo.com/123717964

14.4 Cross area lighting
https://vimeo.com/123717965

15.1 Side, cross and back lighting
https://vimeo.com/123717966

15.2 Focusing lanterns
https://vimeo.com/123718043

16.1 The lighting palette
https://vimeo.com/123718047

16.2 A touch of colour
https://vimeo.com/123718049

17.1 The language of lighting
https://vimeo.com/123718050

Lighting the Show

18.1 Designing the show
https://vimeo.com/123718051

19.1 Which lantern to use & where
https://vimeo.com/123718124

22.1 Lighting a scene
https://vimeo.com/123718126

22.2 Lighting the show
https://vimeo.com/123718125

Technical info. – Lanterns, Dimmers & Control

➤ **Makes & models of tungsten lanterns – a quick guide**

Fresnels, PCs, Profiles, Parcans

Makes – manufacturers	Country of origin	Models – lantern names
Altman Stage Lighting	North America	Fresnels, Ellipsodial, PAR 38/46/56/64, Border lights, Ground & Sky Cyclorama; Comet & Luminaire follow spots
ADB Lighting Technologies	Belgium	Europe range & Warp
CCT Lighting Mainly used in UK educational market	United Kingdom	Minuette, Freedom Eco, Starlette, Silhouette ranges; Freedom follow spot
ETC	North America	Source Four Axial, PAR and Parnel
Philips Selecon	New Zealand	Acclaim, SPX, Pacific, Rama, Arena, Hui & Lui, Aurora ranges; Pacific and Performer follow spots
Robert Juliat	France	'LUTIN', Le CIN'K, SX ranges; Foxie, Ivanhoe and Manon follow spots
Spotlight	Italy	Combi, Sintesi, Evolution, Vendette
Strand Lighting No longer manufacturing lanterns	United Kingdom	Quartet, Prelude, Nocturn, Coda, SL, Brio, Harmony and Cantata ranges
Teatro Teclumen No longer manufacturing lanterns	Italy	Forma, Curva, Atto ranges; Arena follow spots
Thomas Engineering	UK, North America	PAR 36, PAR 56, PAR 64

TECHNICAL INFO. Lanterns, Dimmers & Control

Ellipsodial lanterns

Makes – manufacturers	Country of origin	Models – lantern names
Altman Stage Lighting	North America	Ellipsoidal: PHX fixed focus & zoom 360Q, 3.5Q
CCT	United Kingdom	Freedom 2000 Zoomspot
ETC	North America	Source Four Zoom, Junior, Fixed Focus
Philips Selecon	New Zealand	Acclaim Axial Zoomspot, SPX fixed focus & zoomspot, Pacific Zoomspot, Pacific Fixed Focus & Long Throw
Strand Lighting	United Kingdom	SL Zoomspot, Brio Zoomspot (no longer manufactured)

➤ **Most commonly used tungsten lamps**

T18	T26	T11	T29	GKV600	HPL575	HPL750
500 watt	650 watt	1000 watt	1200 watt	600 watt	575 watt	750 watt
Focus lanterns Altman, CCT, Philips Selecon, Spotlight, Strand				**Axial lanterns** Acclaim, SPX, Pacific, SL	**Axial lanterns** Altman, Source Four	

Lanterns, Dimmers & Control

TECHNICAL INFO.

352

➤ Lantern reference guide

Make	Lantern Model	Wattage	Voltage	Lamp Type	Frame Size	Gobo Holder	Gobo Size
Altman							
Altman	**6" Quarz Fresnel**	750W	120V	T6 120V	7½" x 7½"		
Altman	**8" Quarz Fresnel**	1000W	120V	T7 120V	7½" x 7½"		
Altman	**3.5" Ellipsoidal MT**	500W	120V	EHC	4⅛" x 4⅛"	3.5Q	
Altman	**Shakespeare S6**	600W	120V	HX754	7½" x 7½"	1KL6	
Altman	**4.5" Ellipsoidal**	750W	120V	HX754	6¼" x 6¼"	360Q	
Altman	**PHX Ellipsoidal**	575/750W	120/240V	GLA/HPL	6¼" x 6¼"	PHX-PH	'B'
Altman	**PHX Zoom**	575/750W	120/240V	GLA/HPL	6¼" x 6¼"	PHXZ-PH	'B'
Altman	**360Q Ellipsoidal**	575/750W	120/240V	HP600	7½" x 7½"		
Altman	**3.5Q Ellipsodial**	575	120/240V		10 1/8"X 10 1/8"		
Altman	**6" Ellipsoidal**	550/575W	120V	EHD/GKE 120V	7½" x 7½"		
Altman	**PAR**	500/1000W	120V	PAR 120V			
Altman	**Comet follow spot**	410W	82V	MR-16 82V			
Altman	**Luminator fs**	410V	82V	MR-16 82V			
ADB							
ADB	**Eurospot**	500/650W	240V	GY9.5	125x125mm	SP/GO	DS/DW
ADB	**'A' Range**	500/650W	240V	GY9.5	155x155mm	A6	A56C
ADB	**Warp**	600/800W	240V	G9.5	185x185mm		'B'

TECHNICAL INFO.

Lanterns, Dimmers & Control

353

TECHNICAL INFO. Lanterns, Dimmers & Control

		Power	Voltage	Lamp	Dimensions	Lamp code	Notes
ADB	Europe	1000/1200W	240V	GX9.5	185x185mm		
ADB	Europe	2000W	240V	GY16	245x245mm		
CCT							
CCT	Minuette	500/650W	240V	T18/T26	125x125mm	GH15	'M'
CCT	Freedom Eco	600/800W	240V	HX600/800	190x185mm		
CCT	Freedom 2000	600/800W	240V	HX600/800	190x185mm	Z0120	'A' 'B'
CCT	Silhouette Turbo	1000/1200W	240V	T19/T29	190x185mm	GH01	'A'
CCT	Silhouette	2000/2500	240V	CP92/CP91	190x185mm	GH01	'A' 'B'
CCT	Starlette	1000/1200W	240V	T19/T29	190x185mm		
CCT	Starlette	2000/2500W	240V	T11/T29	190x185mm		
CCT	Starlette Flood	1000/1250W	240V	K4	375x265mm		
ETC							
ETC	Source Four Junior	375/575W	240V	HPL375/575	159x159mm	GH63	'M'
ETC	Source Four Zoom	575/750W	240V	HPL575/750	159x159mm	GH59	'B'
ETC	Source Four fixed angle	575/750W	240V	HPL575/750	159x159mm	GH59	'B'
ETC	Source Four Fresnel	575/700W	240V	HPL575/750	159x 159mm		
ETC	Source Four Par	575/750W	240V	HPL575/750	190x190mm		
ETC	Source Four Parnel	575/750W	240V	HPL575/750	190x190mm		
Robert Juliat							
Robert Juliat	Lutin 306	1000W	240V	CP70/T19	180x180mm		
Robert Juliat	310H Range	1000/1200W	240V	CP70/CP90	215x215mm		

TECHNICAL INFO.

Lanterns, Dimmers & Control

Make	Lantern Model	Wattage	Voltage	Lamp Type	Frame Size	Gobo Holder	Gobo Size
Robert Juliat	329H Range	2000/2500W	240V	CP91/CP92	245x245mm		
Robert Juliat	600SX	1000/1200W	240V	T19,CP70/T29,CP90	190x190mm		
Robert Juliat	700SX2	2000/2500W	240V	CP92/CP91	215x215mm		
Rober Juliat	Aledin 630SX	LED 85W	240V	LED lamp unit	190x190mm		
Philips Selecon							
Selecon	Acclaim	500/650W	220/240V	T18/T25	125x125mm	GH60	'M'
Selecon	Acclaim Axial	600W	220/240V	GKV600LL	125x125mm	GH60	'M'
Selecon	Leko Lite	575/750W 800W	115V 230V	Philips High-Brite			
Selecon	SPX	600/800W	220/240V	GKV600/800LL	185x185mm	GHB	'B'
Selecon	Pacific	600/1000W	220/240V	GKV600LL	185x185mm	GHPB	'B'
Selecon	High Performance	1000/1200W	220/240V	T11/T29	185x185mm		
Selecon	Compact	1000/1200W	220/240V	T11/T29	185x185mm		
Selecon	Rama	1000/1200W	220/240V	T11/T29	185x185mm		
Selecon	Arena	2000/2500W	220/240V	CP92/CP91	245x245mm		
Selecon	Acclaim Cyc/Flood	500W	220/240V	K1 Frosted	230x204mm		
Selecon	HUI	500/800W	220/240V	K1/P211	265x203mm		
Selecon	LUI	1000W	220/240V	K4 Frosted	265x203mm		
Selecon	Aurora	625/1000/1250W	220/240V	P2/10/7/12	305x315mm		

TECHNICAL INFO.   **Lanterns, Dimmers & Control**

		Wattage	Voltage	Lamp		Code	M/B
Spotlight							
Spotlight	**Combi**	500/650W 1000/1200W 2000/2500W 5000W	230V 230V 230V 230V	T18/T26 T11/T29 CP92/CP91	TC S05	PGM 100 PGM 100	'M' 'B'
Spotlight	**Sintesi Arena Sintesi Vario Sintesi Figura**	500/650W 1000/1200W 2000/2500W	230V 230V 230V	T18/T26 T11/T29 CP92/CP91	TC S05	PGM 100 PGM 100	'M' 'B'
Spotlight	**Evolution**	1000/1200W 2000/2500W	230V 230V	T11/T29 CP92/CP91	TC S05	PGM 100 PGM 100	'M' 'B'
Strand							
Strand	**Patt. 23**	500W	240V	T28	100x100mm	GH08	'B'
Strand	**Patt. 123**	500W	240V	T25	165x165mm		
Strand	**Prelude**	500/650W	240V	T18/T26	150x150mm	GH73	'B'
Strand	**Quartet**	500/650W	240V	T18/T26	150x150mm	GH33	'M'
Strand	**Cantata**	1000/1200W	240V	T11/T29	185x185mm	GH06	'B'
Strand	**Alto**	2500W	240V	CP91	245x245mm		
Strand	**Patt. 60 Flood**	500W	240V	GLS Clear	300x300mm		
Strand	**Brio**	600W	240V	HX600	150x150mm	GH06	'B'
Strand	**SL**	600W	240V	GKV600LL	158x158mm	GH73	'B'
Strand	**Coda/Nocturne**	500/1000W	240V	K1/K4 Frosted	215x245mm		
Strand	**Leko**	1000W	240V	CP77			
Strand Century							
Strand	**Leko**	500W	120V	EHD			
Strand	**Leko**	750W	120V	EHG			

Make	Lantern Model	Wattage	Voltage	Lamp Type	Frame Size	Gobo Holder	Gobo Size
Strand	Leko	1000W	120V	CP77			
Teatro							
Teatro	**Forma**	500/650W	240V	T18/T26			
Teatro	**Curva**	650/1000/1200W	240V	T21/T19/T29			
Teatro	**Atto**	2000W	240V	CP55/CP75			
Teatro	**Ribalta**	300/500W	240V	K9/K1			
Teatro	**Linea**	625/1000/1250W	240V	P2/10/7/12			
Zero 88							
Zero 88	**Focus 650**	550/650W	240V	T18/T26	125x125mm		
Thomas							
Thomas	**Par 64**	1000W	240V	CP60 Narrow CP61 Medium CP62 Wide CP95 Ex Wide	254x254mm		

TECHNICAL INFO. Lanterns, Dimmers & Control

Lanterns, Dimmers & Control

TECHNICAL INFO.

Cable connectors

Country	Amps	Volts	Connector name	Pins
United Kingdom	15 amp	230 volts	Cable plugs & sockets	3 pin round
United Kingdom	16 amp	230 volts	CEE P17	3 pin round
Europe	10 amp	230 volts	IEC	3 pin flat
Europe	16 amp	230 volts	CEE P17	3 pin round
Europe, Germany	16 amp	230 volts	Schuko	2 pin round & earth
Australia & New Zealand	10 amp 20 amp	230 volts	3 pin Piggy circuit plug 3 pin Piggy circuit plug	3 pin flat blade
North America	20 amp	120 volts	Edison SPC Stage Pin Connectors	flat 3 in line parallel round pin '3-pin stage cable'
North America	20 amp	120 volts	Edison stage pin	twist lock

- **Amps** are the measurement of the rate of flow of the electrical current in a circuit
- **Volts** are the measurement of the constant electrical pressure or force of the mains supply of the country of origin: UK, Europe, Australia & New Zealand 230 volts, North America 120 volts
- **The size of the connectors** and diameter of the pins depends upon the maximum power handling of the cable being used that is measured in amps
- **16 amp CEE P17** are used in the UK for moving heads with discharge lamp sources to prevent them being connected to a dimmer circuit.[1] They are also used for outdoor installations as the circular body of the male and female connector is fully enclosed when joined together providing a waterproof connection

➤ Dimmer ratings

Country	Voltage	Rating	Dimmer ratings
UK	230 volts	Amps	10A, 16A, 25A
Europe	230 volts	Watts	2.5kW, 3kW, 5kW, 12kW
Australia/New Zealand	230 volts	Amps Watts	10A, 13A, 15A, 25A 2.5kW, 3kW, 5kW, 12kW
North America	120 volts	Watts	600W, 1.2kW, 2.4kW

[1] Moving heads/discharge lamps, see Chapter 6 'DMX fixtures – A quick start – Animated fixtures'

➤ Safe working loads – Power-handling capacity 230 volt supply

Safe 'rule of thumb': 10 amps = 2kW – 15 amps = 3kW – 16 amps = 3.5kW

Mains supply – 230 volts	Dimmer rating amps	Max power watts	Approx load kilowatts	Safe working load no. of lanterns
Dimmer units	10 amps	2300 watts	2kW	3 x 650W lanterns 2 x 1000W lanterns
Dimmer units & sockets	13 amps	2990 watts	3kW	4 x 650W lanterns 2 x 1200W lanterns
Dimmer units, sockets & extension cables	15 amps	3450 watts	3kW	5 x 650W lanterns 3 x 1000W lanterns
Dimmer units, sockets & extension cables	16 amps	3600 watts	3.5kW	5 x 650W lanterns 2 x 1200W lanterns
Dimmer units	25 amps	5750 watts	5.5kW	4 x 1200W lanterns 2 x 2000W lanterns
Mains electrical supply	32 amps	7360 watts	7kW	10 x 650W lanterns 6 x1200W lanterns
Mains electrical supply	63 amps	14490 watts	14kW	20 x 650W lanterns 12 x1200W lanterns
Mains electrical supply	100 amps	23000 watts	20kW	35 x 650W lanterns 19 x 1200W lanterns

➤ Safe working loads – Power-handling capacity 120 volt supply

Safe 'rule of thumb': 10 amps = 1kW – 20 amps = 2kW

Mains supply – 120 volts	Dimmer rating amps	Max power watts	Approx load kilowatts	Safe working load no of lanterns
Dimmer units & extension cables	10 amps	1200 watts	1kW	2 x 575W lanterns
Dimmer units & extension cables	20 amps	2400 watts	2kW	4 x 575W lanterns 3 x 750W lanterns
Mains electrical supply	30 amps	3600 watts	3.5kW	6 x 575W lanterns 4 x 750W lanterns
Mains electrical supply	60 amps	7200 watts	7kW	12 x 575W lanterns 9 x 750W lanterns
Mains electrical supply	120 amps	14400 watts	14kW	24 x 575W lanterns 19 x 750W lanterns

TECHNICAL INFO.

Lanterns, Dimmers & Control

Lanterns, Dimmers & Control

TECHNICAL INFO.

➤ Three phase supply – colour coding

Country	EU/IEC 2004 harmonised colours	UK pre-2004	USA	Canada	Australia New Zealand
Phase L1	Brown	Red	Black	Red	Red
Phase L2	Black	Yellow	White	Black	White – (previously Yellow)
Phase L3	Grey	Blue	Green	Blue	Dark Blue

IEC – International Electrotechnical Commission

➤ Lighting control desks – makes and models

Manufacturer	Country of Origin	Manual Control	Basic Memory Control	Advanced Memory Control
ADB Lighting Technologies	Belgium	**SWING** 6 & 12 cf*	**MIKADO** 12/24 cf **DOMINO** 24/48 cf	**DOMINO/XT** 48/96 cf **HATHOR** cc infinite
ETC	North America	**Smartfade** 12/24 or 24/48 cf	**Smartfade ML** 48 cf 1024 DMX outputs **Element 60** 250/500 cc*	**Congo JR** **Congo** 3072 cc 6144 DMX outputs **Congo Kid** **Ion** 1000/1500/ 2000 cc **Eos** 5000cc **Eos Ti** **Cobalt** 5,000 cc
Jands Pty Ltd	Australia	**Stage 24** 24/48 cf **ESP II** 24 & 48 cf **Event 24 & Plus 48**	**Event 408** 24/48 cf **Event 416** 36/72 cf	**Jands Vista**
LSC Lighting Systems	Australia	**MINIM** 12/24 cf		**maXim** 24 – 120 cf

* cf channel faders/cc control channels

Philips Strand	United Kingdom	**100 series** 12/24 cf	**200 series** 12/24 or 24/48 cf	**preset Palette** 32/64 or 48/96 cf **classic Palette** 150, 250 or 500 cc **Light Palette classic** 800 cc **300 Series** 125 cc **500 Series** 500 cc **Neo** DMX 100 Uni
Zero 88	United Kingdom	**Juggler** 12/24 cf	**Jester & ML** 24/48 cf **Jester TL** 200 cc	**Leap Frog 48 or 96** cf 248 or 296 devices **ORB** 2048 cc
MA Lighting	Germany		**Lightcommander 2** 24/6 48/6 cf	**grand MA2**

Live & moving lights control desks

Avolites	United Kingdom		**Diamond 4 Elite** **Diamond 4 Vision**	**Sapphire** **Pearl** Live control desks
ChamSys 'Cam' 'Sis'	United Kingdom			**MagicQ:** **Expert, Pro,** **Pro Execuite**
High End Systems	North America			**Whole Hog 3** **Road Hog** Specialist moving lights desks
MA Lighting	Germany			**grand MA2**

➢ **Moving heads – makes & models**

Company	Country of origin	Fixtures: MH – Moving Heads
ADB Lighting Technology	Belgium	**WARP/M** motorised Axial zoom Profile **EUROPE** motorised Plano/Prism- convex, Fresnel
Clay Paky	Italy	**Arc-Lamp:** **Alpha, Spot, Wash, Profile** **Supersharpy, Mythos, Shotlight Wash** **A.leda B-EYE K20** LED
Chauvet Professional	North America	**Legend:** **330SR** Spot, **30SR** Beam, **412Z** LED **Rouge:** **R2** Beam, **R2** Spot, **R1** Beam, **R1** Spot **Q-Wash: 419Z** – LED, **560Z** – LED

LEE Dichroic Glass Colours

■ **36** – Colour effects filters and Architectural colours

Apollo Dichroic filters

Few saturated colours, mainly pale and some tints

■ **41** – Colour effects filters and Architectural colours

➤ Makes of gobo rotators

Type/ motor	Single Gobo	Dual Gobo	Double Gobo	Double Gobo	Indexing
Apollo	Smart Move Jr (M)	Smart Move		Smart Move DMX	
Chroma-Q	Junior FX (B)		Twin FX	Twin FX DMX	
GAM		Twin Spin Jr (M) Twin Spin		Dual Motor Twin Spin	
Rosco	Single Rotator	Vortex	Double Rotator	Revo Dual	Indexing Rotator
Control	**Stand alone**	**Stand alone**	**Remote controller**	**DMX**	**DMX**

Technical info. – Lighting the Show

➤ Scales – metric and 'English units'

1:25 metric scale

1mm Drawing size	Represents 25mm Actual (full) size		
1mm	=	25mm	(.025m)
4mm	=	100mm	(.100m)
10mm	=	250mm	(.250m)
20mm	=	500mm	(.500m)
40mm	=	1000mm	(1.000m)
80mm	=	2000mm	(2.000m)
60mm	=	4000mm	(4.000m)
500mm	=	5000mm	(5.000m)

American system scale 'English units' ½" : 1ft

Measurements on the drawing =	Full-size measurement
½" =	1ft
1" =	2ft
2" =	4ft
2½" =	5ft

➤ True length of throw and beam spread from a lantern

True length of throw (metres) – lantern to centre of the area

Vertical height of lantern	3m	4m	5m	6m	7m	8m	9m
10m	10.40	10.70	11.20	11.60	12.20	12.80	13.40
9m	9.50	9.80	10.30	10.80	11.40	12.00	12.70
8m	8.50	8.90	9.40	10.00	10.60	11.30	12.00
7m	7.60	8.10	8.60	9.20	9.90	10.60	11.40
6m	6.70	7.20	7.80	8.50	9.20	10.00	
5m	5.80	6.40	7.10	7.80	8.60		
4m	5.00	5.65	6.40	7.20			

Horizontal depth from lanterns to centre of the area

Beam spread diameter (metres)[3]										
Field angle										
5°	0.3	0.3	0.4	0.5	0.6	0.7	0.8	0.9	1.0	1.1
10°	0.5	0.7	0.9	1.0	1.2	1.4	1.6	1.7	1.9	2.1
19°	1.0	1.3	1.7	2.0	2.3	2.7	3.0	3.3	3.7	4.0
26°	1.4	1.8	2.3	2.8	3.2	3.7	4.2	4.6	5.1	5.5
36°	1.9	2.6	3.2	3.9	4.5	5.2	5.8	6.5	7.1	7.8
50°	2.8	3.7	4.7	5.6	6.5	7.5	8.4	9.3	10.3	11.2
	3m	**4m**	**5m**	**6m**	**7m**	**8m**	**9m**	**10m**	**11m**	**12m**
True length of throw/distance of lantern to centre of the area										

➢ Generic lantern reference guide – Wattage, beam/field angles, optimum throw

Fresnels				
Make	**Lantern Type**	**Wattage**	**Beam Angle**	**Optimum Throw**
Altman				
Altman	**6" Fresnel**	**500/750W**	**4.2ft dia**	@ 21ft – Short
Altman	**8" Fresnel**	**1000W**	**6.3ft dia**	@ 30ft – Medium
ADB				
ADB	**Eurospot**	500/650W	**9°–65°**	Short
ADB	**'A' Range**	500/650W	**9°–66°**	Short
ADB	**Europe** Prism-convex Plano-convex Prism-convex Plano-convex	 1000/1200W 1000/1200W 2000W 2000W	 **7°–61°** **10°–65°** **8°–58°** **5°–65°**	 Medium Medium Long Long
CCT				
CCT	**Minuette** F	650W	**10°–59°**	Short
CCT	**Starlette** F	1200W	**7°–38°**	Medium
CCT	**Starlette** F	2000W	**5°–50°**	Medium/Long

[3] Stage Electrics – Hire & Sales Catalogue 1998

Make	Lantern Type	Wattage	Beam Angle	Optimum Throw
Fresnels				
ETC				
ETC	**Source Four Fresnel**	575/700W	9°–52° 20–50	Medium/Long
Robert Juliat				
Robert Juliat	**Lutin** 6" **Lutin 310H** 8" **Lutin 329H** 8"	1000W 1000W 2000/2500W		Short Medium Long
Interchangeable Fresnel, Pebble & PC lenses available				
Selecon				
Selecon	**Acclaim** F	500/650W	4°–64°	Short
Selecon	**Rama** F	1000/1200W	5°–60°	4M–18M Medium
Selecon	**Rama 175 HP**	1000/1200W	4.5°–62°	4M–20M Medium
Selecon	**Arena** F	2000/2500W	4.5°–60°	6M–25M Long
Spotlight				
Spotlight	**Combi**			
Spotlight	**Com 05 F**	500/650W	7°–62°	Short
Spotlight	**Com 12 F**	1000/1200W	7°–53°	Medium
Spotlight	**Com 25 F**	2000/2500W	7°–65°	Long
Spotlight	**Com 50 F**	5000W	9°–57°	Long
Spotlight	**Sintesi**			
Spotlight	**Area AR 05**	500/650W	7°–62°	Short
Spotlight	**Area AR 12**	1000/1200W	7°–53°	Medium
Spotlight	**Area AR 25**	2000/2500W	7°–65°	Long
Strand				
Strand	**Patt 123**	500W	15°–45°	5M Short
Strand	**Quartet** F	500/650W	7.5°–55°	6M Short
Strand	**Prelude** F	500/650	7.5°–55°	8M Short
Strand	**Cantata** F	1200W	4°–49°	15M Medium
Strand	**Alto** F	2000/2500W	7°–62°	20M Medium/Long
Teatro				
Teatro	**Forma F eco** **Forma F 650**	500/650W 500/650	7°–60° 7°–60°	2–16M Short 2–16M Short

Make	Lantern Type	Wattage	Beam Angle	Optimum Throw
Fresnels				
Teatro	**Curva F eco**	1200W	**10°–56°**	2–18M Medium
	Curva F 1200		**10°–56°**	2–18M Medium
Teatro	**Atto F 2000**	2000W	**10°–70°**	3–25M Long
Zero 88				
	Pebble Con	500W	**10°–59°**	Short

PCs				
Make	Lantern Type	Wattage	Beam Angle	Optimum Throw
Altman – PCs not included in this manufacturer's range of lanterns				
ADB				
ADB	**Eurospot** PC	500/650W	**9°–65°**	Short
ADB	**'A' Range** PC	500/650W	**9°–66°**	Short
ADB	**Europe**			
	Prism-convex	1000/1200W	**7°–61°**	Medium
	Plano-convex	1000/1200W	**10°–65°**	Long
	Prism-convex	2000W	**8°–58°**	Long
	Plano-convex	2000W	**5°–65°**	Long
CCT				
CCT	**Minuette** PC	650W	**10°–59°**	Short/Medium
CCT	**Starlette** PC	1200W	**7°–38°**	Medium/Long
CCT	**Starlette** PC	2000W	**5°–50°**	Medium/Long
Robert Juliat				
Robert Juliat	**Lutin** 6"	1000W		Short
	Lutin 310H 8"	1000W		Medium
	Lutin 329H 8"	2000/2500W		Long
Interchangeable Pebble, PC & Fresnel lenses available				
Selecon				
Selecon	**Acclaim** PC	500/650W	**4°–64°**	Short
Selecon	**Rama** PC	1000/1200W	**5°–60°**	4m–18m – Medium
Selecon	**Rama 175 HP**	1000/1200W	**4.5°–62°**	4m–20m – Medium
Selecon	**Arena** PC	2000/2500W	**4.5°–60°**	6m–30m – Long
Spotlight				
Spotlight	**Vario VA 05**	500/650W	**5°–56°**	Short

Make	Lantern Type	Wattage	Beam Angle	Optimum Throw
PCs				
Spotlight	**Vario VA 12**	1000/1200W	**4°–63°**	Medium
Spotlight	**Vario VA 25**	2000/2500W	**4°–66°**	Long
Strand				
Strand	**Quartet** PC	500/650W	**7.5°–55°**	6m Short
Strand	**Prelude** PC	500/650	**7.5°–55°**	8m Short/ Medium
Strand	**Cantata** PC	1200W	**4°–49°**	15m Medium
Strand	**Alto** PC	2000/2500W	**4°–58°**	20m Medium/Long
Teatro				
Teatro	**Forma PC eco** **Forma PC 650**	500/650W 500/650	**7°–60°** **7°–58°**	2m–16m Short/ Med 2m–16m Short/ Med
Teatro	**Curva PC eco** **Curva PC 1200**	1200W 1200W	**8°–60°** **8°–60°**	2m–20m Medium 2m–20m Medium
Teatro	**Atto PC 2000**	2000W	**9°–70°**	3m–27m Long
Zero 88				
Zero 88	**Pebble Con**	500W	**10°–59°**	Short

Profile Spots				
Make	**Lantern Type**	**Wattage**	**Beam Angle**	**Optimum Throw**
Altman				
Altman	**Ellipsoidal** 3.5"–MT	500W 500W	**18° 23° 28°** **38° 48°**	Short/Medium Short
Altman	**Shakespeare Ellipsoidal** S6 S6-1535Z S6-3055Z	600W 600W 600W 600W	**5° 10° 20°** **30° 40° 50°** **15°–35°** **30°–55°**	Short/Medium Short Short/ Medium Short
Altman	**Ellipsoidal** 4.5"–MT	750W 750W 750W	**15°–30°** **25°–30°** **30°–60°**	Medium Short/Medium Short
Altman	**Ellipsoidal** 6" Series	750W	**6"x 9", 12", 16", 22"**	Medium/Long
Altman	**PHX Ellipsoidal**	575/750W	**5 10 19 16 36 50**	Long Medium

373

Lighting the Show

TECHNICAL INFO.

Make	Lantern Type		Wattage	Beam Angle	Optimum Throw
Profile Spots					
Altman	**PHX Zoom**		575/750W	**15°–35°** **30°–55°**	Long Medium
Altman	**360Q Ellipsoidal**		575/750W	**8.0 8.5 11** **16 22**	Long
Altman	**3.5Q Ellipsodial**		575W	**18 23 38 40**	Long/Medium
ADB					
ADB	**Eurospot**	D54 D54	500/650W	**18°–30°** **30°–47°**	Medium Short
ADB	**'A' Range**	A59Z	500/650	**16°–35°**	Short/Medium
ADB	**Warp**		660/800W	**12°–30°** **22°–50°**	Medium Short
ADB	**Europe**	DW105	1000/1200W	**15°–38°**	Medium/Long
		DS105	1000/1200W	**15°–31°**	Medium/Long
		DSN105	1000/1200W	**11°–23°**	Long
		DN105	1000/1200W	**9°–20°**	Long
		DVW105	1000/1200W	**38°–57°**	Medium/Long
		DS205	2000W	**13°–36°**	Long
		DN205	2000W	**10°–22°**	Long
		DVW205	2000W	**30°–54°**	Medium/Long
CCT					
CCT	**Minuette**				
	Fixed lens		650W	**26°**	Short
	Reflector zoom		650W	**21°–36°**	Short
	Condenser zoom		650W	**17°–36°**	Medium
	Condenser zoom		650W	**30°–48°**	Short
	Condenser zoom		650W	**6°–14°**	Long
CCT	**Freedom**		600/800W	**7°–17°**	Long
			600/800W	**16°–30°**	Medium/Long
			600/800W	**25°–58°**	Short/Medium
CCT	**Silhouette Turbo**		1000/1200W	**11°–26°**	Long
			1000/1200W	**15°–32°**	Long
			1000/1200W	**28°–52°**	Long
CCT	**Silhouette**		2000/2500W	**11°–26°**	Long
			2000/2500W	**15°–32°**	Long
			2000/2400W	**28°–52°**	Medium/Long
ETC					
ETC	**Source Four**	fixed	575W	**26° 36° 50°**	Short
	Junior	zoom	575W	**25°- 50°**	Short

Make	Lantern Type		Wattage	Beam Angle	Optimum Throw
Profile Spots					
ETC	**Source Four** fixed lens		750W 750W 750W	**5° 10° 14°** **19° 26° 36,** **50° 70° 90°**	Long Medium Short
ETC	**Source Four**		750W 750W	**15°–30°** **25°–30°**	Long Medium/Short
Robert Juliat					
Robert Juliat	**600 SX Series**	611 613 614	1000/1200W 1000/1200W 1000/1200W	**11°–26°** **28°–54°** **16°–35°**	Medium Short/Medium Medium
Robert Juliat	**700 SX2 Series**	710 711 713 714	2000/2500W 2000/2500W 2000/26500W 2000.2500W	**10°–25°** **8°–16°** **29°–50°** **15°–40°**	Long Long Long Long
Robert Juliat	**Aledin 630SX**	631 633 634	LED 85W LED 85W LED 85W	**11°–26°** **16°–35°** **28°–54°**	
Selecon					
Selecon	**Acclaim**		500/650W 500/650W	**18°–34°** **24°–44°**	Short/Medium Short
Selecon	**Axial**		600W 600W	**18°–34°** **24°–44°**	Medium Short
Selecon	**Pacific**		600/1000W 600/1000W 600/1000W	**12°–28°** **23°–50°** **90° Wide**	Medium/Long Short/Medium Short/Medium
Spotlight					
Spotlight	**Combi**				
Spotlight	**Combi – Com 05 ZW**		500/650W	**23°–40°**	Short
Spotlight	**Combi – Com 05 ZS**		500/650W	**14°–32°**	Short
Spotlight	**Combi – Com 12 ZW**		1000/1200W	**24°–50°**	Medium
Spotlight	**Combi – Com 12 ZS**		1000/1200W	**13°–35°**	Long
Spotlight	**Combi – Com 25 ZW**		2000/2500W	**17°–36°**	Medium
Spotlight	**Combi – Com 25 ZM**		2000/2500W	**12°–25°**	Long
Spotlight	**Sintesi**				
Spotlight	**Figura – FI 05 ZS**		500/650W	**14°–35°**	Short
Spotlight	**Figura – FI 12 ZS**		1000/1200W	**13°–35°**	Medium

TECHNICAL INFO. Lighting the Show

Lighting the Show

TECHNICAL INFO.

Make	Lantern Type	Wattage	Beam Angle	Optimum Throw
Profile Spots				
Spotlight	**Figura – FI 25 ZS**	2000/2500W	**9°–25°**	Long
Spotlight	**Figura – FI 05 ZW**	500/650W	**23°–40°**	Short
Spotlight	**Figura – FI 12 ZW**	1000/1200W	**24°–50°**	Medium
Spotlight	**Figura – FI 25 ZW**	2000/2500W	**17°–36°**	Long
Spotlight	**Evolution**			
Spotlight	**EVO 12 H ZW**	1000/2000W	**20°–41°**	Medium
Spotlight	**EVO 12 H ZS**	1000/1200W	**12°–24°**	Long
Spotlight	**EVO 25 H ZW**	2000/2500W	**18°–38°**	Long
Spotlight	**EVO 25 H ZS**	2000/2500W	**8°–22°**	Long
Strand				
Strand	**Patt. 23**	500W	**26°**	6m Short
Strand	**Quartet**	500/650W 500/650W	**18°–34°** **24°–44°**	8m Medium 6m Short
Strand	**Prelude**	500/650W 500/650W	**16°–30°** **28°–40°**	8m Medium 6m Short
Strand	**Cantata**	1200W 1200W 1200W	**11°–26°** **18°–32°** **26°–44°**	18m Medium 15m Medium 12m Short/Med
Strand	**Alto**	2000/2500W 2000/2500W 2000/2500W	**8°–16°** **14°–32°** **20°–38°**	25m Long 20m Medium/ Lng 15m Medium
Strand	**Brio**	600W 600W	**18°–30°** **28°–40°**	10m Medium 8m Short
Strand	**SL Zoom**	600W 600W	**15°–32°** **23°–50°**	12m Medium 10m Short/Med
Strand	**SL 5°/10°/19°** **SL 36°/ 50°**	600W 600W	**5° 10° 19°** **36°/50°**	Long Short Medium
Strand	**Leko 11** 8"x13" **Leko 18** 6"x16" **Leko 26** 6"x12" **Leko 40** 6"x9"	1000W 1000W 1000W 1000W	**14°** **21°** **30°** **45°**	Long Long Short/Medium Short
Strand Century				
Strand Century	**Leko 6"x12"**(=L26) **Leko 6"x13"**(=L11)	500/750/1000W 500/750/1000W	30° 14°	Short/Medium Medium/Long

Make	Lantern Type	Wattage	Beam Angle	Optimum Throw
Profile Spots				
Teatro				
Teatro	**Forma**	650W	**10°–28°**	2m–14m Short
		650W	**20°–40°**	2m–12m Short
Teatro	**Curva**	1200W	**8°–22°**	5m–25m Med/L
		1200W	**18°–36°**	5m–25m Long
Teatro	**Atto**	2000W	**8°–22°**	6m–30m Long
		2000W	**18°–36°**	6m–25m Long
Zero 88				
Zero 88	**Focus**	500/650W	**21°–36°**	Short/Medium
			30°–45°	Short

Websites

➤ Lantern manufacturers

www.altmanltg.com	Altman Stage Lighting: NA
www.adblighting.com	ADB Lighting Technologies: Belgium
www.cctlighting.com	CCT Lighting: UK
www.etcconnect.com	ETC: NA
www.seleconlight.com	Philips Selecon: New Zealand
www.robertjuliat.fr	Robert Juliat: France
www.spotlight.it	Spotlight: Italy
www.strandarchive.co.uk	Strand Lighting archive
www.jthomaseng.com	James Thomas Engineering: UK
www.teclumen.it	Teatro Teclumen: Italy

➤ Dimmers & control desks

www.adblighting.com	ADB Lighting Technologies
www.avolites.org.uk	Avolites
www.etcconnect.com	ETC
www.highend.com	High End Systems
www.jands.co	Jands Pty Ltd
www.lsclighting.com	LSC Lighting Systems
www.strandlighting.com	Philips Strand Lighting
www.zero88.com	Zero88

➤ Moving heads

www.adblighting.com	ADB Lighting Technologies
www.etcconnect.com	ETC
www.highend.com	High End Systems
www.claypaky.it	Clay Paky
www.martin.com	Martin Professional
www.vari-lite.com	Philips Vari-Lite
www.qmaxz.com	Qmaxz Lighting
www.robelighting.com	Robe Lighting

➤ LED fixtures

www.adblighting.com	ADB Lighting Technologies
www.chroma-q.com	Chroma-Q
www.etcconnect.com	ETC
www.martin.com	Martin Professional
www.pixelrange.com	Thomas Engineering
www.robelighting.com	Robe Lighting

www.robertjuliat.fr	Robert Juliat
www.vari-lite.com	Philips Vari-Lite
www.seleconlight.com	Philips Selecon
www.spotlight.it	Spotlight

➤ Health and Safety

www.hse.gov.uk/publications	HSE – Health and Safety Executive
http://ladderassociation.org.uk	The Ladder Association
www.pasma.co.uk	PASMA – Prefabricated Access Suppliers' & Manufacturers' Association
www.scottint.com	Scott Health & Safety Bump Hats

➤ Access systems

www.zargesuk.co.uk	Zarges Skymaster ladder
www.escauk.co.uk	ESCA UK
www.airborne-ind-acc.co.uk	Instant UpRight Span towers
www.tallescope.co.uk	Tallescope – Aluminium Access Products Ltd

➤ CAD – Computer aided design

www.autodesk.com	AutoCAD
www.cast-soft.com	CAST Software Ltd, wysiwyg
www.modelboxplans.com	CAD lantern symbols for use on AutoCAD
www.nemetschek.net/spotlight	Vectorworks Spotlight

➤ Colour filters

www.leefilters.com	LEE Filters
www.rosco.com	Roscolab
www.gamonline.com	GAM Products
www.apollodesign.net	Apolo Design & Technology

➤ Associations

www.abtt.org.uk	ABTT – Association of British Theatre Technicians
www.ald.org.uk	ALD – Association of Lighting Designers
www.usitt.org	USITT – United States Institute for Theatre Technology
www.theatrestrust.org.uk	The Theatres Trust
www.womeninlighting.com	WISE – Women in Stage Entertainment

Websites

LIGHTING RESOURCES

➤ Stage lighting equipment & hire UK

www.aclighting.com	A.C. Lighting Ltd – High Wycombe Bucks
www.ajs.co.uk	AJS Theatre Lighting & Stage Supplies – Ringwood, Hampshire
www.black-light.com	Black Light Ltd – Edinburgh
www.centraltheatresupplies.co.uk	Central Theatre Supplies – Birmingham
www.hawthorns.uk.com	Hawthorn – Leicester
wwww.kave.co.uk	Kave Theatre Services – West Sussex, Derbyshire
www.lancelyn.co.uk	Lancelyn Theatre Supplies – Oxford, Merseyside
www.northernlight.co.uk	Northern Light – Edinburgh
www.productionireland.com	Production Services Ireland – Belfast
www.nstage.co.uk	Northern Stage Services Ltd – Oldham
www.stage-electrics.co.uk	Stage Electrics – Bristol, London, Tyneside
wwww.whitelight.ltd.uk	White Light (Electrics) Ltd – London

➤ Stage lighting equipment & hire global

www.aclighting.com	A.C. Lighting Ltd – Toronto Canada
www.gamonline.com	GAM Products – Los Angeles USA
www.apollodesign.net	Apollo Design & Technology – Fort Wayne IN, USA

➤ Equipment & accessories UK

www.flints.co.uk	Theatrical Chandlers (Quad spanners and Caritools)

➤ Additional training resources

www.stagelightingtraining.co.uk	'Give Me Some Light!!!' DVDs and student resources
skipmort@stagelightingtraining.co.uk	Skip Mort Stage Lighting Training – educational resources

➤ 'Give Me Some Light!!!'

Three interactive lighting workshops on DVD for students providing self-directed study, support for examination coursework options GCSE, A2 & BTEC, fast-track training, health & safety and teachers' Continued Professional Development.

Key notes!

➤ Make a note of what you have done

You will be asked to provide curriculum vitae when you make an application for a job or a place on a college course. CVs are a brief account of your education and experience, in other words what you have done. It can be quite useful to start making a list of the types of equipment that you have used, any specialist courses that you have taken, the shows that you have worked on and the roles that you have been responsible for.

Lanterns used

Make	Model	Type	Make	Model	Type

Lighting control desks

Make	Model	Familiar with	Can use	Plotted & run show

Live & moving lights desks: e.g. Sapphire, Pearl, Hog, grand MA

Make	Model	Familiar with	Can use	Plotted & run show

Specialist courses	Organising body – certification	Date
Working at heights		
Using access equipment		
Risk assessment		
Electrical testing		

Shows		
Date	Show	Role/responsibility

Industry contacts – people you have met or worked for		
Name	Position	Theatre/company

> ➤ **Make a note of the contacts that you have made**

Trade contacts			
Company	Contact	Phone number	Website

> ➤ **Notes**

LIGHTING RESOURCES **Credits**

Credits

Online video link Resources

Extracts from '**Give Me Some Light!!!**'
Three interactive stage lighting workshops on DVD for students. 'Need a Technician', 'Taking the Drama out of Lighting!' & 'So You're Lighting the Production?'

Written & directed by Skip Mort
Assistant director & presenter Andy Webb
Filmed & edited by Mike Hill – an Attic Studios production
© SKIP MORT LIGHTING SERVICES 2005

The making of the original DVDs were sponsored by Philips Selecon, Roscolab, Zero 88, ESCA, Stage Electrics, and supported by Strand Lighting, LEE Filters, CCT Lighting UK, Skyhigh FX, Scott Health & Safety.

Other contributions

Article on 'War Horse' video design by Julie Harper for Lighting & Sound International (www.lsionline.co.uk)
Designers on Colour – Guide to Colour Filters Roscolab
Introduction to DMX by David Whitehead – Stage Electrics
Electricity – how does it work? by David Whitehead – Stage Electrics
Swan Lake – lighting the transformation scene – Rick Fisher
Lighting the shows – *Swan Lake* & *Billy Elliot* – Rick Fisher
CAD Programs used for Stage Lighting – David Ripley – Royal Central School of Speech & Drama
Designing a larger show – *Our House* – Andy Webb

Production photographs

Photographs of Tigz Productions – Nik Sheppard www.sheppardphotography.com
Uncle Vanya, Birmingham Repertory Theatre – Robert Day
Billy Elliot – Tristram Kenton
War Horse – Simon Annand
Hamlet, *Berlin 2006*, *Decadence* – Andrew Malmo
Crazy Mary – Brain Aldous
'Give Me Some Light!!!' – Skip Mort

Product photographs

Reproduced by courtesy of:
ABTT Sightline – Bob Morgan
ALD-TTV Technologies
Altman Lighting

Apollo Design Technology, Inc. – Apollo Gelbook
Avolites
Chauvet Professional
Clay Paky
Colin and Lindsey Ockwell – St Augustine Theatre
ESCA
ETC
GAM Products Inc
High End Solutions
Instant UpRight
Le Maitre – Pyrotechnics & Special Effects
LEE Filters – Art of Light
MA Lighting
Martin Professional
Philips Selecon – Performance Lighting
Philips Strand
Philips Vari-Lite
Robe
Roscolab Ltd – Product Guide, Guide to Colour Filters, Guide to Motion Effects
Spotlight
Stage Electrics
Strand Electric – Education in Stage Lighting
Thomas Engineering
Thomas Nell – LED lighting images and illustrations
White Light
Zarges UK
Zero 88 Cooper Controls – Product Guide

Drawings

Michael Mackie-Clark, Kave Theatre Services – LxDesigner plans
Steve Shelly – Selecon lantern stencil drawing
Sam Tanner – wsyiwyg plans

Bibliography

2011 Code of Practice for the selection and use of temporary access equipment for working at heights in the theatres – ABTT

2014 Code of practice for use of Tallescopes for working at heights in theatres – ABTT

'All The Worlds a Stage' – Thomas Nell, Spotlight

Alpha 300/700 Product Guides – Clay Paky

Apollo Design Technology inc. website – www.apollodesign.net

Basics – A Beginners Guide to Stage Lighting – Peter Coleman

'Calculating power' – Virgina Tech. www.the12volt.com/ohm/ohmslaw.asp

Chromarange catalogue – Pulsar Light of Cambridge Lighting, Hire & Sales

'Code of Practice for In-Service Inspection and Testing of Electrical Equipment' – The Institution of Electrical Engineers

Current trends in video design for theatre – Sightline ABTT, Dick Straker

Educational Guide to Stage Lighting – Strand Lighting

'Electrical Maintenance including Portable Appliance Testing' – The Institution of Electrical Engineers

'ETC's Source Four LED v2' – Rob Halliday, Lighting & Sound International plasamedia

Five steps to risk assessment – HSE UK

GAM Products inc. website – www.gamonline.com

Health & Safety, Risk Assessment – Central School of Speech and Drama

Hire & Sales Catalogue 1998 – Stage Electrics

Intro to Stage Lighting – Steve Marshall, www.seleconlight.com

Introducing projected computer images – Teaching Drama, Paul King

Jands Vista Control desks – Neil Vann Jands Europe

Lantern information – Philips Selecon

MAC TWI Product Guide – Martin

Making of War Horse – More 4

Martin Professional website – www.martin.com

Moving Effects Catalogue – DHA Lighting

Performance Lighting Design – Nick Moran

Pixel Range – LED Lighting – www.pixelrange.com, Thomas Engineering

Rosco Guide to motion effects – Roscolab

Rosco Product Catalogue – Roscolab

Scene Design & Stage Lighting – W. Oren Parker & Harvey K. Smith

Selecon beam angles data – Philips Selecon

'Sensor: Coming of Age as More Than Just Dimming' – et entertainment technology

Stage Lighting Design – Bill Williams

Step into the Limelight – Strand Lighting Drama Resource Pack

Strand Electric, Rank Strand, Strand lighting Luminaires – Brian Legge, ABTT Archaeology Committee

The Art of Light – LEE Filters

The Art of Stage Lighting – Frederick Bentham

The Hire Store Catalogue – Stage Electrics

The Strand Archive – www.strandarchive.co.uk

Theatre Craft – www.theatrecrafts.com
Theatre Projects – resources – Theatre Projects website
'Thrusting, Flexible and Green – Royal Shakespeare Theatre' – A K Bennett-Hunter, ABTT 'Sightline' Jounrnal of Theatre Technology and Design
War Horse – Lighting & Sound International – Julie Harper
'White Light and PTB make ENO a UK First with ADB TwinTech Dimming' – et entertainment technology
White Light Catalogue reference section – White Light Entertainment
Wikipedia the Free Encyclopaedia – www.wikipedia.org
Zero 88 Product Guide – Cooper Controls

Index

Accent lighting 254, 255
Alice in Wonderland 184–5
'Allo 'Allo 246, 334–5
Angling lanterns 19, 35
Animation discs 165, 169–70
Automated fixtures 93–4
   Scrollers 93
Automated lighting rigs 99, 328
Automated yoke lanterns 98
Axial Ellipsoidal Profiles 28

Back lighting 207, 236–8, 246
Barndoors 21, 236
Base down Ellipsoidal Profiles 29
Beam spread 298, 296–7, 368–9
Berlin 260
Billy Elliot 270–1
Black light 202

Cable connectors 38, 357
CAD computer programs 284–6, 312, 317
Chief electrician 276
Colour 144–8, 219–230, 239
   Complementary 148
   Effects of 256
   Primary 147
   Secondary 148
   Temperature 113
   Using 250–1, 252–7
Colour frames 22
Colour filters 364–6
   Cutting 136–7
   Diffusion139–40
   Filter materials 139–20
   Identifying 135–6
   LED filters 141
   Plastic 123
   Ranges 140–1, 364–8
   Storing 137
Comedy of Errors 267
Computer software 285–7
Crazy Mary 255
Cross area lighting 228–9
Cross lighting 233–4, 236, 246
Cyc Floods/light 10, 24, 101, 299

Dance, lighting for 247–8, 243
Decadence 260
De-rigging lanterns checklist 36
Design team 276
Dichroic break-ups 162–4
Dichroic glass filters 365–6
Digital projection/images 181–4
   Front & rear projection 182–3
   HD integrated moving digital lights 186
   Projecting moving image 186
   Projection screen materials 185
Dimmer packs 5, 56, 58–9, 222
Dimmer racks 4–5, 55, 223
Dimmers 4, 55–8
   Hard patching 66
   Hardwired systems 66
   Power-handling capacity 57–8
   Ratings 57, 357–8
   Replacing a fuse 58
Director 276
Discharge lamps 46–7, 97, 147
Dissolves 203
DMX 512 63, 83, 89–92, 93–4
Donuts 21
Drama, lighting for 245–6
Dress rehearsal 337
Dry ice 196

Electrical equipment, testing 50–1
Extension cables, coiling 37

Face, lighting 216, 256
Field/beam angle 292–3
Fill lighting 253–4
Flat area lighting 226–7, 246
Floods 10–11, 24, 101–2
Floor lighting 235–6
Focus lanterns 11–12, 19–22, 35
Focusing moving fixtures 327
Fog 191–3, 197–9
   Machines 198–9
FOH lighting 231
   Layers of light 239
Fresnels 11–12, 21, 25, 225, 242, 294, 296, 297
Front lighting 217, 226–7, 236, 252

Gauzes 203–5
Gobo rotators 166–7, 171–75
  Cloud 173
  Effects 171–4
  Fire smoke 173
  Makes of gobo rotators174
  Reflection of sunlight on water 174
Gobos 20, 153–60, 162–3, 169, 174–5
  Controllers 174–5
  Dichroic break–ups 162–3
  Forest and woodland effects 159
  Glass 153, 162
  Graphics 155
  Making plastic slides 179
  Non-realistic patterns 155
  Projecting images 171
  Projecting plastic slides 177–8
  Realistic projected patterns 155
  Stained glass window 159
  Stainless steel 153
  Window gobo 158
  Working with 154
Groundrow 24

Hamlet 237
Haze 191–3, 195–7
Head lighting 240, 246
Health & Safety 117–19, 125–8
  Access systems 119
  CO_2 197
  Electrical safety checklist 117–18
  Pyrotechnics 207–8
  Risk assessment 125–8, 361–2
  Smoke & fog machines 199
  Strobe lighting 201
  Tallescopes 120
  UV light 202
  Working at heights 118
  Working with lanterns 118
High-level cross lighting 236
High School Musical 249

Incandescent lamps 45, 97, 147
Institution of Electrical Engineers 50
iPro image projector 177
Irises 20

Key lighting 253, 254

Ladders 120–1
  Combination 121
  Extension 120
  Step 120
Lamps bases, types of 43
  Replacing 43–4

Types of 45
Lanterns/luminaires 3, 9–13
  CIE symbols 13
  Cleaning 41
  Design 30
  Makes and models 15–16, 348–53
  Range of 291–2
  Reference guide 368–9
  Rigging 33–5
  Selecting 291
  Stencils 289
  Troubleshooting 42–3
  Types of 9–13
  Wattage 15–16
Larger shows, lighting 310–17
  Creating a cue list 339
  Fit-up, the 222–3
  Focusing 323, 326–7
  Preparation 338
  Programming fixtures 338
  Rigging 324–6
Layers of light 239
LED fixtures 106–8
LED Performance moving heads 104, 106
LED Technology 111–12
  Monochromatic whites 112, 113
  Performance luminaires 101–5
  Prism mixing 114
  Reflection
  Technology 111–15
  x7 Colour chip sets 113
Light, source and direction 213–6
Lighting control desks 77–86
  Advanced memory control desks 83–4
  Crossover lighting desks 85–6
  Integrated lighting desks 84
  Live lighting desks 85
  Makes and models 332–3
  Manual control desks 77–9
  Memory control desks 81–2
Lighting designer (LD) 276
Lighting layout plan 279–81, 289–90
Lighting programmer 338, 340
Lighting rehearsal 336
Lighting thrust stage 239
Lightning effects 202
Liquid CO_2 196

Magic sheet 318
Mains electrical supply power capacity 62–3
Metal halide lamps 45, 147
Miniature circuit breaker (MCB) 60, 61
Moving lights/fixtures 954–5
  Automated yoke lanterns 94
  Digital moving heads 96